SHERMAN'S 1864 TRAIL OF BATTLE TO ATLANTA

Mercer University Press
1400 Coleman Avenue | Macon, Georgia 31207
www.mupress.org

MUP/P220

First Edition

The paper used in this publication meets the minimum requirements
of American National Standard for Information Sciences—
Permanence of Paper for Printed Library Materials, ANSI
Z39.48-1992.

Library of Congress Cataloging-in-Publication Data

Secrist, Philip L.
The Sherman trail of battle to Atlanta, 1864 | Philip L. Secrist
1st ed.
p. cm.
Includes bibliographical references and index.
ISBN-13: 978-0-86554-745-2 (pbk. : alk. paper)
ISBN-10: 0-86554-745-9 (pbk. : alk. paper)
1. Atlanta Campaign, 1864 | I. Title.
E476.7.S34 2006 | 973.7'371--dc22

2006017049

SHERMAN'S
1864 TRAIL OF BATTLE TO
ATLANTA

PHILIP L. SECRIST

MERCER UNIVERSITY PRESS | 2006

Sgt. Philip M. Secrist, 10th Virginia Infantry, 1863.

Sgt. Secrist's memorial plaque in Kennesaw GA.

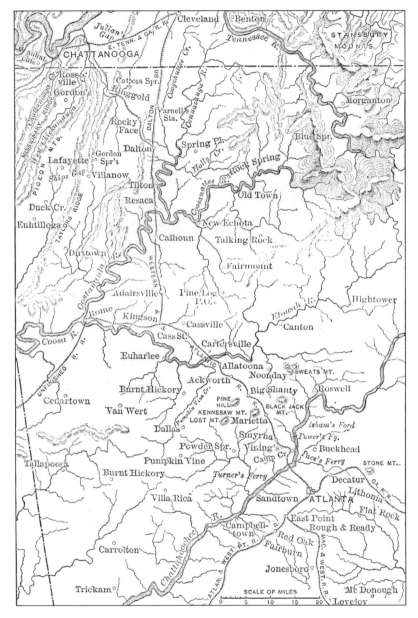

Map of the route of the Atlanta Campaign from Jacob D. Cox's book, *Atlanta*. Cox was a division commander in the 23rd Army Corps throughout the Atlanta Campaign and went on to a distinguished career in politics and business. Published shortly after the war, Cox's *Atlanta* is generally considered the best single source for the tactical story of the campaign.

CONTENTS

RATIONALE AND ACKNOWLEDGMENTS

—•◦•—

This book is the result of a special interest in military history by a teacher whose professional career began in 1955 in Atlanta, Georgia. I am that teacher. Whatever special touch this effort may bring to the better understanding of the military story of the Atlanta Campaign is found in my interest in historic preservation and my concern that the character of the battlefield terrain be a major consideration in any analysis of leadership and tactical results. My experience in the Marines and in the Army infantry taught me the value of terrain and environment in the conduct of battle. I learned it was important to examine the "lay of the land" as a better way to understand the flow of battle and the command decisions (or lack of) made at time. While it is imperative to bring academic research and writing skills to such a project, placing the historic event within the context of its action-environment through extensive on-site examinations is equally important and most often ignored by academicians.

So it was that over a period of nearly fifty years this curiosity has led to countless days spent on "ridge and ravine," metal detector and shovel in hand, searching for traces of marching armies and battling regiments. Some of the evidence of military action gathered through the years from these sites is pictured at appropriate points in this book. The quest for a better understanding of tactical decisions by commanders has led me to search for many forgotten or unmarked battlefields. It has been for me a personally rewarding career of discovery, enlightenment, and adventure. Among those whom I met whose interest in the Atlanta Campaign also focused on place and location was Wilbur G. Kurtz, gifted artist and historian. Mr. Kurtz, Illinois native, came to Atlanta in the early 1900s, married the daughter of Captain William Fuller of the Andrews Raid story, and began a life-long historical devotion to the story of Atlanta's experience in the Civil War. His maps and research will be used wherever possible throughout this narrative.

Another valuable resource in this work has been Franklin Garrett. Mr. Garrett's remarkable product of research on the subject of nineteenth-century Atlanta, a book entitled *Atlanta and Environ*, published nearly fifty years ago is still the beginning point for study of the early story of the city. His lifelong devotion to the history of his adopted city and his leadership in preserving its past should be remembered.

And Kennesaw State University student, Jeff Frederick, should be recognized as a major research contributor and co-author of the chapter regarding the acquisition of the state historic site of Pickett's Mill battlefield. Mr. Frederic engaged in extensive personal interviews with state officials in the Georgia Department of Natural Resources in Atlanta in 2002. Of special importance was Frederick's success in gaining the trust and cooperation of the senior department historian, Mr. Billy Townsend. Townsend was present and personally involved during the entire period of the state's acquisition and development (1971–1976) of the Pickett's Mill historic site. The inside political maneuvers and tactics of public officials and the responses from the department staff are especially interesting.

INTRODUCTION

———◆•◆———

The Atlanta campaign of 1864 would have been impossible
without this road [Western and Atlantic Railroad], that all
our battles were fought for its possession, and that the
Western and Atlantic Railroad of Georgia should be the
pride of every true American because by reason of its existence the Union was saved. Every foot of it should be
sacred ground, because it was moistened by patriotic blood,
and that over a hundred miles of it was fought a continuous
battle of 120 days, during which, day and night, were heard
the continuous boom of cannon and the sharp crack of
the rifle.

—*William T. Sherman, General*

A primary purpose of this narrative is to describe the happenings
and attempt to capture some of the drama associated with the
series of military events along the 100-mile battle route of General
William T. Sherman's 1864 Atlanta campaign in tour guide fashion. To
accomplish this we will rely on a knowledge of the geography of the
route, use personal accounts by the military and civilian participants, and
utilize period and modern photographs and maps associated with the
sites. Additionally, as we visit these places along the battle corridor we will

comment on the current level of public interest in each and its present state of preservation.

Let us make the case for historic preservation. In 2004, we commemorated the 140th anniversary of the Battle of Kennesaw Mountain in my home county. We have in our community a 3,000-acre national park dedicated to that event and its numerous sacrifices. Out of this battle, and scores like it, that generation of Americans who endured the Civil War forged a more perfect union.

Conflict is often the product of competing beliefs and convictions, sometimes destructive, always controversial, and occasionally productive of new strengths. Many conflicting forces are at work in our country today, and these forces will alter the physical face of our communities and determine the course of our history. At my home in Cobb County, Georgia, in metro-Atlanta, change comes so quickly we seem to have little time to reflect on the extended impact it will exert on our personal lives and well being.

For instance, we are told to expect great population increases in Cobb County in the next few years. What price must we pay for absorbing double our present population in such a short period of time? Is the county to be substantially deforested to make room for this population growth? What hills will be leveled and lakes drained, or new lakes created? What skylines will change? What roads will have new lanes added, curves straightened, grades reduced or new roads built, to improve, we are told, the flow of traffic?

We say this is progress, but at what price "progress"? What must we lose to make these gains that are said to go with urban growth? Is it really possible to enjoy a healthy economic growth and yet retain a measure of the poetry and grace of a life rich in the substance and fullness of pleasant surroundings? It is these surroundings, we should remember, that reflect the enduring strength of basic human values that have stood the test of time.

Each generation is the product of cumulative social and cultural forces producing specific historic experiences, which, past and present, have shaped each generation, and which are at work even now on our own. In short, we remain the product of past circumstances and present forces and pressures. How do we deal with this? In a storm, we seek anchors to hold to—enduring and tested anchors.

Certainly our religious faith is important. We also achieve a sense of inner peace and comfort in the certain and familiar—in a wooded hill or valley that conveys a sense of serenity and beauty or serves as a personal reminder of some perceived happier time. A historic house or the ruins of a long-ago military fort or grist mill convey the comfort of knowing the certainty of the outcome of past events, while at the same time, in our own lives, we cannot now know the conclusion to our daily experiences.

The lesson of history is "perspective"—the long vision. Thus we learn patience in dealing with our daily encounters; the lesson that today, or some day, "this too will pass!"

The tangible evidence of a historic event is important. As a wise man once said, each generation will not be judged so much by what it builds, but rather by what it does not destroy.

So we now find ourselves at a crossroads in Cobb County as well as in the nation. What is the useful past? Which and what of the natural beauty of our hills and streams should be preserved? Cobb County was a battleground for nearly six weeks of military activities 139 years ago—a national experience, the American Civil War.

The events of the summer of 1864 seem remote in 2004, but what of the cumulative consequences of the human experiences at Fort Hood, Gilgal Church, Latimar's Farm, Manning's Mill, the Green Plantation, Pine Knob, Ruff's Mill—and Kennesaw Mountain? Why should we be concerned about preserving the Cheney House on Powder Springs Road, where General Sherman planned the battle of Kennesaw Mountain, or marking the spot in the Due West community where the Indiana brigade of future President Benjamin Harrison fought hard at Gilgal Church, or setting aside some ruins of military fortifications on the Kennesaw-Due West Road where Arthur MacArthur, the father of Douglas MacArthur, led his Wisconsin regiment in combat?

What purpose is served with such concerns? Why not forget it all? Is there usefulness in preserving tangible evidence of past events? I think so.

I know we must be concerned if we hope to preserve our identity as a united people consciously sharing the bond of our common historical past. It is a uniting and strengthening experience for a community to share a sense of heritage. But while we share this common bond, we have the responsibility not to judge events of the past romantically, or judge by the values of the present. To do so is to deal ignorantly, unfairly, and arrogantly with the past; to foolishly set aside the lessons to be learned, and to misjudge and misuse history and its symbols.

Case in point is the misuse of the symbol of the Confederate battle flag. The St. Andrews Cross with its thirteen stars became the best known of the Confederate battle flags—it became a symbol of great human courage and sacrifice in a "Lost Cause." The popular inspiration of the times that produced this flag was concerned more with the constitutional question of the nature of the union than with the perpetuation of slavery.

All this has been forgotten or never learned by some bigots who display the flag at their public occasions and by those who in justified outrage have come to despise the Confederate battle flag as the symbol of racism. The entire debate is all so foolishly wrong and it is a misuse and misunderstanding of our historical experience.

How sad it was to see a few years ago the small crowd and the absence of media attention on the occasion of the burial in Marietta of a Civil War soldier whose remains lay in their 1864 battlefield burial site until discovered by accident. It would appear that somehow the fate of this nineteen-year-old unknown Confederate soldier, honored in this recent graveside ceremony by so few people and the battle flag that draped the simple pine coffin, had become an embarrassment to the community in which he had given his full measure of devotion. Whether we like it or not, that historical event did happen. And whether we like it or not, the process of history and change is at work with us today.

Cobb County will complete its cycle of urban transition—this is certain, and there will be ample opportunity in the immediate years ahead for economic gain by the sensitive developer who is committed to quality work. Our county and our country will confront the issues of urban land use alternatives, of development, of density, of transportation needs, of waste disposal and water supply—and at the same time consider the preservation of the most desirable characteristics of our county's landscape and historical heritage.

As we seek the necessary balance during this critical time, we shall as individuals and as a community be required to make the difficult decisions that will become a statement of our personal and community values for future generations to see—and for history to judge.

The purpose of this narrative is to suggest a route of travel today along an 1864 path of historical events which to that generation of participants was an intensely personal daily experience. Because large numbers of these soldiers in both armies had a remarkable degree of literacy, we are able to catch a glimpse through diaries and letters, of the human emotions of the occasion as they faced the challenges of their very personal military experience in 1864. And by following the route of march we can share the story as they tell it; and in many instances visit the actual scenes of battle on hills, in thickets, and across streams where action took place as described in the story of each person's personal "long road to Atlanta."

As the journey begins along the 1864 battle corridor the first stop is Ringgold, Georgia. Here, as Sherman assembled his army for the great campaign, he surely gazed southward toward distant Atlanta with many apprehensions. Roads to Atlanta today are well marked and paved; this of course was not the case in 1864—only the Western and Atlantic Railroad could be the army's dependable lifeline throughout the 120-day campaign. Today our concerns are not that of an army commander, but rather an interest in history and its preservation. As we travel southward we are impressed by the abundance of historical resources still present and by the wealth of good roads accessing these sites. First among these roads remains the state-owned 1864 right-of-way of the original Western and Atlantic Railroad once used by Sherman. And conveniently nearby is Interstate 75 constructed in the 1960s running in many instances parallel to the railroad battle corridor. Additionally there are well-maintained state and county roads giving convenient access to the more remote sites.

Adding on-site interest to many of these points are small memorial parks constructed in the 1930s by the Works Progress Administration (WPA). These pocket parks commemorate nearby military activity and remain in place today as attractive and educational points of interest along the trail. These reservations are now owned by the Georgia

Department of Transportation but are often maintained by the local community. Encouraged by such facilities along the battle route, we can also be pleased by the evidence of mounting support for historical preservation from the general public, and we must be appreciative as always for the dependable support of such natural allies of preservation as "Friends" groups, Civil War roundtables, reenactor organizations, historical societies, and Sons and Daughters of Confederate veterans organizations. Our journey today begins south of Tunnel Hill at the site of the winter camp of the Confederate army at Dalton in spring 1864.

The Clisby Austin House in Tunnel Hill. This was Sherman's headquarters during the first week of the Atlanta Campaign in May 1864.

The pre-Civil War Ringgold railroad station is still in use today as a community welcome center. This building was badly damaged by Federal artillery in November 1863, in the Battle of Ringgold.

The 1864 railroad tunnel at Tunnel Hill GA. A key military site in the Atlanta Campaign, it shared history with the nearby Clisby Austin House. The tunnel was retired in the 1920s due to increasing size of locomotives and rolling stock. A larger tunnel was built nearby. The 1864 tunnel was restored with federal and state grant money in the 1990s. The wartime railroad station is nearby.

1

MILITARY ACTIVITIES
NEAR DALTON

———•◦•———

Major General Hugh Weeden Mercer, West Point graduate and Savannah banker, brought his brigade of four Georgia regiments to Dalton in early May 1864. While the 1,400 men in Mercer's brigade may have been pleased to have missed the cold winter in Dalton, they had also missed a much-needed reorganization in supply and equipment, drills in military command and leadership, and site-specific tactical training provided by veteran officers of the Army of Tennessee now under the direction of the new Confederate commander Joseph E. Johnston. Mercer's brigade would learn war the hard way—on the march and in the trenches.

General Johnston had been appointed to command the army earlier that year and set about doing the job with a blend of compassion, strict discipline, and common sense that soon won over the troops. In fortifying the approaches to Dalton, Johnston included flooding Mill Creek at the railroad pass and entrenching the hills in the valley north of town. The rugged range of mountains west of Dalton called Rocky Face, through which Mill Creek flowed, served nicely as a natural defense. With artillery placed properly to protect the approaches to Mill Creek Gap, a few pickets south of town at Dug Gap, and fortified hills north of town, Johnston felt comfortable that Dalton was safe from attack. In truth it was—and Sherman would use this reality to his advantage in the first of his great flanking moves to trap the Confederate Army of Tennessee.

Mercer's brigade had been transferred from the Department of South Carolina and Georgia in late April and assigned to W. H. T. Walker's division of Hardee's corps of the Army of Tennessee. Other regiments were being gathered throughout the Deep South to fill out the ranks of the undermanned Tennessee army. Along with these other untested units, Company I, 63rd Georgia Regiment, Mercer's brigade, soon learned that hometown garrison duty had indeed been poor preparation for the demands of a military campaign. On 9 May, while on picket duty in Mill Creek Gap, the regiment was roughly handled by forward elements of Sherman's advancing veteran infantry. Captain Charles W. Howard's Company I (63rd Georgia) was spared total embarrassment only because nearby regiments came to their aid. The next few days would bring a procession of bone-wearying new challenges to the men of the Georgia 63rd.[1] Marching through Dalton that night on the road to the small railroad village of Resaca 13 miles south of Mill Creek Gap, Howard's men of the 63rd would follow their "Old Captain" to what would be the first great test for General Johnston's Confederate army.

The "Old Captain" was fifty-three-year-old Charles W. Howard. A graduate of the Theological Seminary at Princeton, New Jersey, his life had combined scholarship with Presbyterian ministry. A co-founder of Oglethorpe University near Atlanta, he had been sent to London in 1837 by the Georgia legislature to obtain copies of the colonial records of Georgia. While there, he had witnessed the coronation of Queen Victoria. After serving a pastorate in Charleston for several years, he bought land in North Georgia along the Western and Atlantic Railroad near Kingston and built the home he called "Spring Bank." Here in 1852, he opened a select school for the sons and daughters of the planter aristocracy living nearby along the Etowah River valley. This already distinguished career in ministry and education was to be cut short by war.

In Savannah where Howard had enlisted in 1862 in the 63rd Georgia Regiment, there had been few military emergencies—hardly preparation for the experience he would face at Dalton in 1864. His men had elected him captain of Company I and began calling him the "Old Captain."

The historic Spring Bank, home of Rev. Charles W. Howard near Kingston GA. His daughter, Frances Howard, wrote the book *In and Out of the Lines* from this home, telling of wartime troubles of private citizens in a war zone. Spring Bank was built in 1840, but burned in 1974.

Captain Howard had reported to his new camp at Dalton after a brief visit with his family at Spring Bank. While realizing that the route of battle that summer would likely threaten his family and engulf his home, and failing in his attempt to persuade the family to refugee south, Howard felt somewhat consoled that the welfare of the family would be in good hands with his twenty-one-year-old daughter Frances in charge—she was spunky; she could hold her own with any Yankee she was likely to encounter. And for now, he must concentrate on his military duties.

These duties began in early May. Some weeks before, General George H. Thomas, commanding the Army of the Cumberland, alerted Sherman to the opportunities offered by Snake Creek Gap as a route by which the rugged terrain at Dalton could be avoided and the railroad reached south of Dalton thus turning Johnston's position and forcing the Confederates to give battle to protect their line of rail supply.[2] Thomas had offered to lead his fast-stepping Cumberland soldiers through this defile while

Sherman's armies of the Ohio and the Tennessee occupied Johnston's attention at Dalton. Sherman accepted the suggestion, but because of transportation delays to the Army of the Tennessee en route from Mississippi he chose to modify the plan by reversing the roles of the Cumberland and the Tennessee armies. The mission of James B. McPherson's Army of the Tennessee was to strike quickly near Resaca via Snake Creek Gap—his movements would be screened by the high ridges west of Dalton while the Cumberland army threatened Dalton at Mill Creek and Dug gaps.[3] Sherman wired Grant on 4 May that he planned to capture Tunnel Hill just west of Mill Creek Gap "then throw McPherson rapidly on his [Johnston's] communications [blocking the railroad at Resaca], attacking at the same time in front cautiously and in force."[4] McPherson with 20,000 infantry was to leave his camp near Rossville, Georgia on 5 May and, in a rapid sweep around the Confederate left via Villanow and Ship's Gap, secure the pass at Snake Creek near Resaca by 7 May. From his position at Snake Creek Gap, he was to make an attack on the railroad near Resaca where a fortified blocking position might be established and held at all costs until the balance of Sherman's army closed in from two directions via Snake Creek Gap and the direct wagon road from Dalton. The maneuver, if successful, would trap the Confederate army against two rivers. "Make the most vigorous attack possible," Sherman wrote McPherson on 5 May, "as it may save us what we have most apprehend—a slow pursuit, in which he gains strength as we lose it."[5] As it turned out McPherson's effort was a failed mission. Successfully passing through Snake Creek Gap without being detected, his 20,000 man Army of the Tennessee emerged from the gap less than 5 miles west of Resaca and the railroad, 13 miles to the rear of the Confederate army in Dalton, and facing only a single brigade of defenders. Blocking the railroad and forcing the Dalton Confederates to attack on grounds of McPherson's choosing should have been a simple matter. Instead, after failing in a half-hearted effort to reach the railroad, the Army of the Tennessee withdrew the same day to Snake Creek Gap and encamped. This event and the events of the next few days would serve to remind Sherman of his own shortcomings, and the limitations of many of his key subordinates. Cumulatively, Sherman's cautiousness in the immediate days ahead would produce a parade of missed opportunities which would force him from time to time to revise his plans and priorities for the campaign.

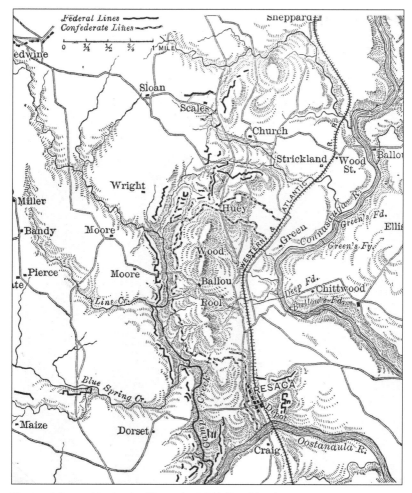

The trench lines and landmarks of Resaca battlefield (Cox, *Atlanta*).

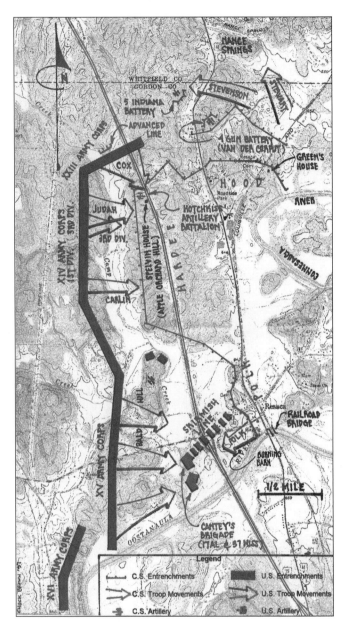

Resaca battle line near Camp Creek where most of the action took place on 14 May 1864. The state of Georgia was able to purchase this portion of the battlefield and preserve it as a state historic site.

BATTLE OF RESACA

The rough and hilly farmland around Resaca was interspersed in 1864 with thick underbrush. Slicing through this landscape, the Western and Atlantic Railroad crossed the Oostanaula River at Resaca on its journey northward from Atlanta to Chattanooga. The village had been named by the workers who constructed the railroad in the 1850s, some of whom were veterans of the Battle of Resaca de la Palma in the Mexican War. By 1864, Resaca had grown to only a few dozen structures clustered about the freight station. Small farms dotted the surrounding country-side, and west of town lay a narrow valley through which flowed Camp Creek. Southwest of the village the creek emptied into the Oostanaula river. Hills and ridges of medium ruggedness formed a border to this valley, following generally a north-south pattern and conforming roughly with the flow of the creek. About a mile north of the village, the railroad swept sharply off to the east where it paralleled for a short distance the southward-flowing Conasauga River—a broad stream which joins the Coosawattee River just east of town to form the Oostanaula on its west-ward journey, skirting the village on the south. Some 3 miles north of the Resaca depot, the railroad again resumed its northerly route to Tilton, Dalton, and beyond. It was in this rectangle formed by the creek and the rivers, and dissected by the railroad, that the battle of Resaca was fought on 14 and 15 May 1864.

Early on the morning of 14 May, both armies were in place, the Federal's north and west of Resaca, their flanks resting at or near the Oostanuala and Conasauga rivers. The Confederate army (many of whom had marched the 13 miles from Dalton during the night) was anchored with its flanks and rear to the same rivers, embracing the village and the railroad bridge within its perimeter, but with its rear and flanks against the river there was no place to run should there be a Federal breakthrough. On 14 and 15 May the battle of Resaca became the first major struggle of the Atlanta campaign.

The heaviest action on the 14th was along the Camp Creek valley west of the village. Here late in the day, elements of McPherson's XV army corps rushed across the creek capturing a forward line of low hills occupied by Cantey's undermanned brigade of Polk's corps, giving the Federals an excellent artillery position from which they could harass the Confederate railroad and foot bridges. Despite repeated attempts, lasting until nearly 10:00 P.M., Polk's efforts to regain these hills were unsuccessful. The Federals now had a key position from which they could interdict the Confederate bridge crossings on the Oostanaula. Earlier that day, supported by a brigade of the XIV Corps, two divisions of the Army of the Ohio failed in their attack on Hardee and Hood near the head of Camp Creek a mile of so north of McPherson's action. Further east along Hood's line, the Confederate division of Brigadier General Carter Stevenson succeeded for a time in driving elements of the IV Corps from the direct wagon road to Resaca but were turned back by the heroics of the 5th Indiana Artillery led by Captain Peter Simonson, the timely arrival of Federal reinforcements, and the coming of darkness. So closed the significant action on 14 May.

On 15 May, battle resumed along Hood's line north of the village. Hooker's XX army corps prepared an attack designed to drive Hood's corps toward the Oostanuala. Poorly managed, Hooker's brigades ran directly into an oncoming Confederate attack equally bungled. Stopped in his tracks by this collision with opposing forces, Hooker did manage to capture a four-gun Confederate battery run too far in advance of infantry by the direct orders of General Hood.

Meanwhile, south of the Oostanaula River, General W. H. T. Walker's division, close to the town of Calhoun, guarding the flank and rear of the Confederate army along the river, had become the victim of a successful river crossing by elements of McPherson's XVI army corps at Lay's Ferry on 14 May. Walker notified Johnston of this threat to the line of retreat, but later sent a second message telling of the Federal withdrawal back across the river near dark. Early the next morning (15 May) the Federal river crossing was repeated, this time with a full division and the construction of a "tete-de-pont" (entrenched beachhead) on the Calhoun side of the Oostanaula River. Out front as skirmishers was the 66th Illinois Regiment many of whom were equipped with the new sixteen-shot Henry rifles.[6] When opponents advanced too close, this unit displayed "a stubborn resistance, and a steady, cool fire, check[ing] the enemy's advance."[7] One captured Confederate told of his experience with the 66th Illinois that day on the skirmish line near the river:

> He saw a "Yank" and at the same time the "Yank" saw him, and each took to a tree. Soon he thought he saw a chance for a shot and fired. Then, he said, that "Yank" just opened up and fired thirteen shots into my tree and the bark and dirt flew powerful; then he called out, "Surrender or I'll fire a volley into you." I certainly thought if he were going to fire a volley after those thirteen shots, I had better surrender. So I came out and he took me in. What kind of guns have you all got, anyway?[8]

An unfired Henry cartridge and copper cases from the Cobb County and Bartow County battle sites.

The Confederate railroad supply line was less than 3 miles away. The Federals were now too strongly entrenched to be attacked. Walker's division was in trouble, and by extension, Joe Johnston's Confederate army. No alternative remained but to retreat.

The Henry rifle saw rather extensive use in the Atlanta Campaign, especially in the battles of Kennesaw Mountain and Allatoona. Large quantities of copper cartridge cases have been recovered from these battlefields.

THE CONFEDERATES
ESCAPES THE TRAP

——◦◦◦——

Assistant Adjutant-General Pollok B. Lee of the Army of Tennessee notified Johnston at 6:00 P.M. on 15 May that there is a "very good crossing now [pontoon bridge] at this place [near the railroad bridge on the Oostanaula River] for every arm of the service," but recommended that no wagons should cross until after nightfall for stealth and security reasons.[9] The Confederate withdrawal from Resaca the night of 15 May was flawless. Hardee's plan of retreat is an example. He instructed that all supply wagons, ambulances, and artillery were to cross on the pontoon bridge, all foot troops (except the skirmishers covering the retreat) were to cross on the railroad trestle bridge (now floored) beginning at 10:00 P.M.—in a Cleburne, Cheatham, and Bate sequence, with thirty-minute departure intervals between each division. Since Walker's division of Hardee's corps was already south of the river near Calhoun guarding the ferry crossings, he was not involved in the river crossing. Walker's job was to protect the flanks and rear of the retreating army. At 1:00 A.M., Hardee's skirmishers were to be withdrawn under the supervision of staff officers from each division. After crossing the river each division was to take up their "ordnance train, ambulances, and artillery."[10] Hood's and Polk's corps extracted themselves from the battlefield during the night equally efficiently. By 5:00 A.M. the field of battle at

Resaca was completely abandoned by the Confederates. As for the Federals, the chase was on.

Cleburne's division would be needed to assist Walker's on 16 May in a rear guard action about 2 miles west of Calhoun at the Rome Crossroads near Oothkaloga Creek. Federal Colonel Elliot W. Rice commanding the 2nd Division, XVI Army Corps, Army of the Tennessee, had abandoned the beachhead at Lay's Ferry on 14 May, reestablished it the next day, but was then reinforced on 16 May by the balance of Brigadier General Granville Dodge's XVI army corps. He now headed for Calhoun and the long train of Confederate supply wagons. Only Cleburne's infantry reinforcements and his judicious placement of a section of rifled artillery on Rice's flank effectively stopping the threat, allowed the retreating Confederates to pass safely through Calhoun. Walker's division had not particularly distinguished itself on the picket line near Lay's Ferry on 14 or 15 May, even losing a battle flag. A daring Federal private had paddled across the river, captured the unprotected flag, and swam back under the covering fire and cheers of his admiring friends.[11]

4

Preservation
of the Battlefield

———◆◆◆———

Not a pound of provisions, not a cartridge, not a gun, not a man, was found to tell the tale. By daylight Johnston's whole force was safely beyond reach, the pontoons taken up, the other bridges dismantled.[12]

A Federal officer described the retreat of the Confederate army from the trap at Resaca during the night of 15/16 May 1864 as a clean escape without "haste, loss, or confusion."[13] For a few more days the battlefield at Resaca would be a busy staging place for the pursuit and for battlefield cleanup details. On 16 May, Benjamin Harrison's Indiana regiment remained on the battlefield for battlefield cleanup. It was their duty to aid in burying the dead and collecting abandoned arms and property of the departed armies.

The battlefield around Resaca bore evidence of the great struggle that had taken place. Thickets of brush, even great saplings, were literally mown down by the storm of musket balls, shot, shell, grape, and canister.[14] A member of another regiment assigned to the same duty noted that trees and bushes were barked and slivered in a manner to indicate that the Federal fire had been terrific, especially at the point where the four pieces of artillery had been captured. Some years after the war, a former officer with the 33rd New Jersey visited the site of his most vivid memory of Resaca:

[T]he little pines were then trees. I found the salient where the battery was, and near it a great long open trench, evidently not a breastwork, for the earth was thrown from it on either side. "What is this?" I asked of the native guide; "This was not here when we fought the battle." "Oh no," said he, "the Yanks buried their dead in that trench. A few years ago they took them up and reburied them in the National Cemetery at Marietta." I have an old canteen with a bullet crease on one side, which I picked up at the open trench that day. Very likely the bullet which creased the canteen killed the man who was carrying it, and the canteen was buried with him in the ditch, and when the bodies were removed, it was left on the ground.[15]

Today, despite the encroachments of a modern interstate highway, the scars of battle remain on the hills near Resaca, mute testimony to the contest waged there so long ago. Here, time-worn breastworks, including a chest-deep earthen embrasure where a future American president would lead his Indiana soldiers in a dramatic and successful effort to capture a Confederate artillery battery, a few iron and lead relics from the

Photograph of the 14 May Camp Creek battlefield taken by George Barnard in 1864. This portion of the battlefield was purchased by the state in 2000.

field and woods, and several surviving photographs from the camera of Civil War photographer George Barnard who in 1864 captured for eternity the poignancy of a forgotten soldier's grave amidst a battle-scared landscape, all combine to remind us that this is hallowed ground. Visiting the Resaca battlefield in the years following the Civil War was made especially convenient because of the continuing passenger service of the state-owned railroad connecting Chattanooga and Atlanta—the wartime Western and Atlantic Railroad. For many years the railroad management promoted passenger travel between the two cities through detailed and colorful tourist pamphlets which extolled the adventure of visiting historical points of interest along the path of Sherman's 1864 Atlanta campaign.

Among other activities associated with the immediate post-war history of the Resaca battlefield was the graves recovery effort by the Federal government searching the fields and woods for the scattered burial sites of *Union* soldiers. A corresponding effort was made at this time by Southern citizens and state officials searching for the remains of *Confederate* casualties. The Federal government went about this task by letting contracts to private contractors on a "cash bounty per remains" basis with very little field supervision by government officials concerning the work of private contractors. As a result, the remains of soldiers were often haphazardly identified as either Federal or Confederate (depending usually on the military buttons found with the remains).

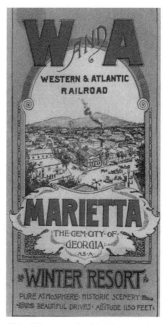

This Western & Atlantic tourism bulletin promoted travel between Atlanta and Chattanooga to visit Civil War sites along the way.

Sometimes in their haste to collect the bounty, contractors did not include all the skeletal remains at the burial site. The box containing the remains was then taken to the nearest national cemetery for certification and bounty collection. Thus because of poor government supervision, bounty collector haste and greed, and the difficulty of the certain identification of individual remains (because of the absence of metal "dog tags" as in World War II), our national cemeteries are now filled with "Unknown Soldier" burials and mixed Federal and Confederate graves. Even today, human remains are regularly found by land developers on construction sites that were once battlefields.[16]

The cost of collecting Confederate remains found at the Resaca battlefield and other battlefields in the South was borne locally with some help from state funding. Largely though, the effort to recover Confederate dead was accomplished through the initiative of local citizens, quite often under the leadership of wives, mothers, and sisters of the fallen. As a direct result of these efforts by Southern women the Confederate Cemetery at Resaca was established.[17] Similar cemeteries sprang up throughout the South. Ultimately, the annual ceremonies at these burial grounds honoring the memory of those who had fallen fighting for the "Lost Cause" resulted in the designation of 26 April (date of the surrender of the last major Southern army) as Confederate Memorial Day. These annual memorial services still continue into the twenty-first century in many Southern states.

In the nearly century and a half since the battle in 1864, remarkably little has changed in the physical appearance of the battlefield. The village of Resaca today remains small, and several families in the community can trace their ancestors to those living in the vicinity in 1864. Small farms and cattle pastures comprise the land use today of much of the battlefield. Ernest Rutledge remembers growing up near Resaca and filling his pockets with lead bullets and shell fragments after every plowing or heavy rain.[18]

The Civil War Centennial in the 1960s, and especially the military technology of World War II that produced the "mine detector" sparked a renewed interest in the history of the Civil War. By 1946, the military mine detector would be available to the public, producing a new generation of collectors of "battlefield iron." Since this metal detector was heavy and cumbersome, and difficult to repair, and since it worked best on

The Resaca Confederate Cemetery established in 1866 through the efforts of Mary Green (left) and others. The Greens' home was used as a field hospital by both sides. The city of Resaca maintains the cemetery today.

Another view of the Resaca Confederate Cemetery as it looked in 2003.

ferrous metals and in low-mineral content ground, the demand for something better stimulated the arrival of a new generation of detectors which began to appear in the early 1960s. These new "high-tech" instruments weighed less than 10 pounds, were easily repaired, and could detect *all* metals at greater depths. The battlefield at Resaca became a favorite hunting ground for the few who read the battle story in the *Official Records*, or for those who had grown up in the nearby community.

An organized interest for the preservation of the Resaca battle field as a deserving historic site began with a remarkable bit of information in 1995—1500 acres of the battlefield was for sale. The newly created Georgia Civil War Commission[19] went into action upon learning of the availability of the battle site. The commission immediately contacted the owner and approached private foundations in order to obtain the necessary funding. Since the idea was that any battlefield property obtained by the commission would go to the state as a permanent historic site, Lonice Barrett, (director of the Georgia Department of Natural Resources under whose management the site would fall) showed his support from the beginning by attending all such meetings, giving his encouragement and in one instance providing a large sum of matching public money to obtain a large private grant. More than $3 million were raised in this manner, followed by a difficult and lengthy process of purchase negotiations with the owners. At last in 2000, the state of Georgia acquired more than 500 acres of the battlefield. All things combined, the acquisition protects nearly the entire western half of the Resaca battlefield along Camp Creek including the entrenchments of Federal and Confederates on the ridges overlooking the valley on each side of Camp Creek. This site, soon to be opened to the public, has been enhanced recently by site-planning grants from the American Battlefield Protection Program. The battlefield project has had support from the local community through a group called "Friends of Resaca Battlefield" comprised of heritage-minded Resaca citizens, and by the support of Resaca officials. Despite the disappointment of getting less acreage then originally hoped for, the preservation story at the Resaca battlefield remains an unqualified success. Much of the process could be consulted as a preservation model for Georgia.

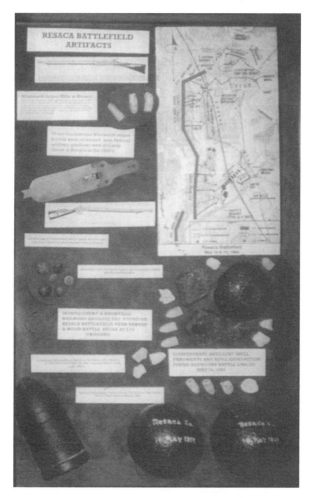

Various recovered items from the Resaca battlefield, including Confederate Whitworth sniper bullets (top) and Federal and Confederate cannon munitions (bottom).

THE RETREAT: POOR ROADS
AND WORSE MAPS

The terrain south of Resaca becomes more open; broad and fertile fields replace the slate-covered hills and mountain ranges found between Dalton and Resaca. In such topography there is opportunity for military chase and attack. As the Federal pursuit began, Jefferson C. Davis's division of the XIV Army Corps was sent forward directly to Rome, some 30 miles southwest of Resaca to destroy or capture the productive Noble Brothers weapons foundry in that town. On 18 May, after a brief fight with few casualties, the factory and its valuable machinery were captured, together with great quantities of baled cotton nearby.

Meanwhile a few miles northeast of Resaca, in following the departing Confederates, John Schofield's XXIII army corps had marched eastward, crossing the Conesauga River at Fite's Ferry and the Coosawattee at Edwards Ferry, then turning southward headed directly toward Adairsville. These military units used all available wagon roads toward this once-peaceful village on the Western and Atlantic Railroad. Joseph Hooker's XX army corps had followed Schofield's route south from the battlefield until reaching the Coosawattee River, at which point Hooker crossed at McClure's Ferry 3 miles west of Edward's Ferry, then turned south taking the direct road to Adairsville. At Fite's Ferry on the Conesauga, while Schofield and Hooker ferried their wagons and artillery over in a small flat-boat, their infantry forded the river stripped naked, carrying their clothes and arms upon their heads "and making great sport of the ludicrous appearance of the column."[20]

Neither of these columns had a pontoon bridge. The only bridging equipment was with the main army at the railroad near Resaca and at Lay's Ferry a few miles downstream. Confusion ruled the day. Due to errors in maps or in the transmission of messages, Hooker's corps instead of crossing the Oostenaula at Newtown (New Echota) on 16 May as intended, crowded in on Schofield's assigned route, seriously encumbering the progress of both corps and forcing Schofield to make a night march in order to place his army at the desired spot near Adairsville on the 18th.

In still other river crossings near Resaca, two divisions of the Federal XIV Army Corps (James B. McPherson's Army of the Tennessee), and the IV Army Corps (Army of the Cumberland) bridged the Oostenaula upstream from Lay's Ferry, west of Calhoun, then moved south and east along the main road toward Calhoun. Two corps of the Army of the Tennessee crossed the Oostenaula at Lay's Ferry and took a road west of the railroad leading south toward Kingston by way of the village of Hermitage and the magnificent plantation "Woodlands" of Godfrey Barnsley. The eventual point of convergence and concentration for Sherman's army was intended to be Kingston. Here the railroad from Rome joined the mainline Western and Atlantic. It was here at Kingston, Sherman reasoned, that the Confederates would surely give battle.

The retreat of Johnston's Confederate army from Resaca along the railroad southward to the Etowah River continued to be a masterpiece of military planning and execution. After successfully crossing the Oostenaula River at Resaca in the early morning of 16 May, the Confederates retreated toward Adairsville, beginning each day's march in the pre-dawn hours, and occupying with retreating columns all roads within reach that ran parallel to the railroad. By so doing, Johnston kept his army marching at a steady pace, moving without haste, while at the same time protecting his flanks from surprise attack.

Typically, Sherman in taking up the pursuit would also begin his march long before dawn and by 8:00 A.M. his columns usually overtook the Confederate rearguard which "immediately showed a bold and determined resistance, behind fences, walls, or barricades of any kind, opening artillery and seeming ready for battle."[21] The Federal forces were thus forced to deploy for battle, an exercise requiring time, giving the Confederates main columns opportunity to put still greater distance between themselves and their pursuers. By the time the Federals were ready to advance in line of battle the Confederate rear guard would vanish. By mid-afternoon this operation was usually repeated if the Federals once again got near, always with the same results. Thus by nightfall Johnston would have his main army far enough away to ensure a peaceful rest, while "Sherman's people were tired and vexed at these unsuccessful maneuvers. Day after day this was done—to our great disgust."[22]

Much of the frustration in both armies was caused by the absence of good maps. The maps available in Georgia in 1864 did little more than represent the outline of the counties, with names of the towns and approximate location of the smaller streams seemingly "drawn at random, as if to fill up the sheet, and were uniformly wrong."[23] The country roads were as misplaced as the streams and so out of scale as to make it impossible to calculate distances between points for the purpose of planning troop movement. To remedy this, the Federal army began a daily mapping program. Each division commander designated a competent officer as a cartographer who reported to the engineers at corps and army headquarters. These officers were instructed to sketch all roads, hills and streams, woods and open land. Local families were questioned, and their "homes noted on these maps as reference points"; much information concerning distances, etc., was gathered in this way. Reconnoitering parties equipped with a few instruments which could be carried on their person systematically gathered such information, which was consolidated and connected, maps being sketched each day, and "by a simple photographic process they were multiplied and distributed to the proper officers of the command."[24] These maps were updated almost daily as new information was discovered. Today, in addition to reliable topographical information, these military maps furnish the historian a great deal of information concerning historic roads, fields, and wood patterns in 1864, and especially valuable, the individual family locations at the time.

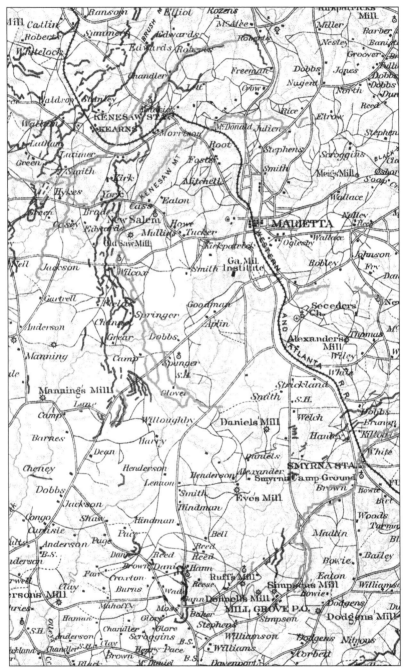

Map illustrating the detail and accuracy of Sherman's map making skills.

ADAIRSVILLE:
THE FIGHT AT THE
OCTAGON HOUSE

---◦◦◦---

Hardee's rearguard action at Rome Crossroads on the 16th had allowed the wagon trains time to clear Calhoun and make the escape southward to Adairsville. Just north of Adairsville, Sam Watkins and others of the 1st Tennessee Infantry Regiment of Maney's brigade (Cheatham's division), serving as rearguard, found themselves in a footrace with Federal soldiers for the protection of an octagon-shaped brick house owned by a R. C. Saxon:

> [A]n order came for our regiment to occupy an octagon house in our immediate front. The Yankees were about a hundred yards from the house on one side and we about a hundred yards on the other. The race commenced as to which side would get to the house first. We reached it, and had barely gotten in when they were bursting down the paling of the yard on the opposite side. We ran to the windows, up-stairs, down-stairs [sic] and in the cellar. The Yankees cheered and charged, and our boys got happy.[25]

The Confederates had orders to hold the house to the last. Soon running low on ammunition, two of their members volunteered to run the gauntlet of lead, successfully returning with a box of 1000 cartridges. The battle raged on until the Confederates withdrew at midnight taking their thirty dead and wounded casualties with them. Watkins described the scene at the house:

> [T]hese casualties were a strange contrast with the furniture of the house. Fine chairs, sofas, settees, pianos and Brussels carpeting being the death-bed of brave and noble boys, all saturated with blood. Fine lace and damask curtains, all blackened by the smoke of battle. Fine bureaus and looking-glasses and furniture being riddled by the rude missiles of war. Beautiful pictures in gilt frames, and a library of valuable books, all shot and torn by musket and cannon balls. Such is war.[26]

Kurtz painting of the fight at the Octagon House. Kurtz painted this pictured based on interviews in the early twentieth century with people who had seen the house. The house was torn down by Federal troops the day after the battle. Bricks from the home may still be found at the site.

It was here at Adairsville, approximately midway between Calhoun and Kingston, that Sherman devised a plan of pursuit that he hoped would force battle and at the same time deprive the Confederates of further use of the Western and Atlantic Railroad. At Kingston the railroad takes a direction due east for almost 5 miles, turns southward again near Cassville, traveling southeast through Cartersville and then crossing the Etowah River and resuming its progress toward Atlanta. Using Thomas's Army of the Cumberland "to follow the broad, well-marked trail of Johnston's army" in its retreat along the railroad southward from Adairsville toward Kingston, and steering his XXIII and XX army corps on different roads east and south via Cassville toward Kingston, Sherman expected to trap the Confederate army in a great pincer movement, severing their rail supply to Atlanta and defeating their army. Instead, for the only time in the Atlanta Campaign, Sherman "the hunter" became the hunted. Assuming incorrectly that the entire Confederate army had retreated along the railroad toward Kingston, he was unaware that Johnston had prepared a trap of his own. Marching from Adairsville on roads leading directly south to Cassville, Hood's and Polk's portions of the Confederate army had arrived at Cassville on 18 May, the day before the arrival of the XXIII and XX Federal Corps. Hardee's large corps, leaving a plain trail, and having indeed retreated southward along the railroad, down the Hall Station road past Captain Howard's home at Spring Bank, would be in position east of Kingston to slow the main Federal army long enough for Polk and Hood to destroy the XXIII and XX Corps near Cassville. This was the plan—here at Cassville the Confederates would have their grand opportunity to defeat Sherman.

When the 63rd Georgia of Walker's division of Hardee's corps marched by Spring Bank early morning on 17 May, the "Old Captain" had a few moments with his family before rejoining his company as it passed. Daughter Frances, in her book *In and Out of the Lines* tells what happened a few hours later with the arrival of the pursuing Federal army. The first Federal soldier coming by spoke civilly and passed on. The next arrival was Federal General Oliver Otis Howard and his staff and escort. Howard came into the veranda with several of his men, sat down, drew out a map and began to ask questions of Frances: the number of

The Western & Atlantic Railroad depot at Adairsville survived the war. The sketch (top) is from *Harper's Weekly*, 1864, while below is how the depot appears today.

Confederates passing by, the individual names of military units, etc. When she answered evasively, the general was annoyed. "He sprang from his chair and, with flushed face, exclaimed: 'Madam, when you meet a gentleman, treat him as such!' We looked silently at each other and he quietly left the veranda."[27] After the general left, the frightened Howard family locked themselves in an upstairs bedroom. They could hear intruders downstairs:

The Yankees thundered up the stairs. Our door was locked, but the others were open, and we heard them throwing down articles of furniture. At last there came a pause, followed by a tremendous blow upon our door, which instantly flew open. The entry and rooms beyond were full

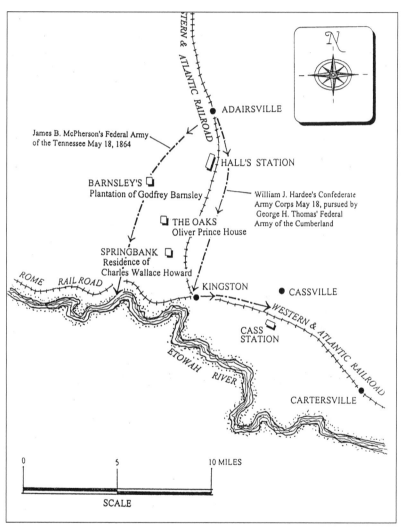

A map by Bill Scaife of Hall Station Rd. near Kingston, Georgia. Spring Bank and Barnsley Gardens are also marked.

of Yankees, many of them half naked at the door. To our great delight we saw a lieutenant walk in, and it is he who had spoken. After expressing his regret that we had been so roughly treated, the lieutenant said he thought the house unoccupied, but as he was passing one of his men told him there were ladies in it, and he had come to investigate.[28]

To prevent further intrusions, a Federal soldier was assigned to guard the Howard home for the next few days.

Five miles northwest of the Howard home was Woodlands, the plantation of Godfrey Barnsley. Forward units of McPherson's Federal Army of the Tennessee had arrived on 18 May, a cavalry skirmish had chased the few Confederate horsemen away leaving one dead rebel leader in Barnsley's garden courtyard.[29] Barnsley, an Englishman and successful cotton factor and ship owner from Savannah, had bought several thousand acres here in the 1850s with a dream of building a magnificent villa for his family. His wife was Julia Scarborough whose family was considered Savannah monied aristocracy. Being English, Barnsley was opposed to African slavery—his Irish domestic and field help at Woodlands were wage servants. The labor used to build the mansion were skilled craftsmen from Pennsylvania. Barnsley lived with his family in a temporary structure at the site while construction was in progress; work was delayed from time to time awaiting building supplies, and Barnsley was often away on business in Savannah and New Orleans. When the war came in 1861, the house and the beautiful grounds at Woodlands were essentially complete. Barneley's two sons enlisted in the Confederate army and he, having now embraced the Southern cause, invested his fortune in Confederate bonds. Sixty-three-year-old Geoffrey Barnsley was living alone with servants at Woodlands when McPherson's soldiers arrived.

The march route taken by McPherson's XV and XVI corps from Lay's Ferry headed toward Hermitage but camped short of there on 17 May at a crossroads called McGuires. From there, on 18 May, while a portion of the of the two corps continued on to Hermitage and then southeast to Woodlands, another column marched due east to Adairsville, then south to Woodlands where they camped for the night. McPherson accompanied the Adairsville column, spending the night as a guest at Woodlands. It is this night that "Biddy" Flannagin (Barnsley's housekeeper) observed that McPherson was "a gentleman, but wan [sic] that's in mighty low company."[30]

Various depictions of Woodlands (present-day Barnsley Gardens).

The Woodlands and Spring Bank Mansions

The months ahead would be difficult for Godfrey Barnsley and his neighbors, the Howards at Spring Bank. Over the next several weeks Barnsley's elegant estate at Woodlands attracted a constant stream of Federal soldier "riff-raft" looking "upstairs, downstairs, and in the garden" for anything of value. On one occasion a soldier asked Barnsley for the time of day—the trusting Barnsley pulled a gold watch from his pocket to oblige, only to have it taken by the ruffian. The soldier then proceeded to the basement, bent on more mischief, but with the outraged, broom-wielding Irish housekeeper in close pursuit. At the foot of the stairs the two had a final confrontation of broom, fingernails, and gun butt "free-for-all" with the Irish woman the loser. But "Biddy" Flannagan was no quitter. Putting on a bonnet, she walked the 3 miles to Kingston, demanded to see the Federal officer in command, told him the story, and was allowed to identify the soldier, which was not difficult to do with "Biddy's" fresh scratches on his face. When Barnsley's gold watch was then produced by this now thoroughly chastened soldier, "Biddy's" revenge was complete. Upon being asked by the commanding officer if he should have this renegade shot by firing squad, "Biddy" thought that her fingernails had extracted enough of his blood for one day. The soldier was punished by being assigned to a labor detail near Chattanooga for the duration of the war.[31]

As the years passed after the war, the Barnsley family and their Woodlands plantation experienced hard times. Barnsley was never able to rebuild his fortune, dying in New Orleans in the 1870s. Descendents struggled unsuccessfully to maintain the estate. A tornado destroyed the roof of the main building shortly after the turn of the century, and Woodlands, land, buildings, and furnishings, were sold at public auction in 1941.

Today, the ruins and surviving structures of the original buildings are owned by a German businessman who has spent considerable money to stabilize the ruins of Woodlands and promote "Barnsley Gardens" as an historic site and upscale weekend golf retreat. Open to the public with admission fees, the rich history at Woodlands seems reasonably well protected for the foreseeable future.

As for Spring Bank, the Howards continued to reside there after the war and into the twentieth century. Returning from the war, Charles Wallace Howard and son-in-law, George H. Waring, began a reasonably successful family business, the Howard Hydraulic Cement Works, manufacturing construction cement from lime mined from the hills across the road from Spring Bank. At the peak of its operation it employed 80 full-time workers and produced 100 barrels of cement daily. Because the product was of superior quality it was used in the construction of the courthouse, post office, and custom buildings in Atlanta, the Union Depot in Chattanooga, East River Bridge in New York, and campus buildings at Shorter College in Rome, Georgia, to name a few.[32] This mining community came to be called Cement, Georgia, complete with US post office and a public school for the children of the workers. At nearby Spring Bank, Frances "Fanny" Howard and her sisters for many years conducted an upscale academy for those few who could afford it. Martha Berry, founder of Berry College in Rome, Georgia, was a student of the Howard sisters. Artist Everett Julio (1843–1879) the accomplished painter of *The Last Meeting of Lee and Jackson* on the eve of the Battle of Chancellorsville, was an instructor at Spring Bank for a short time, and is buried in the small Howard cemetery nearby. Fanny Howard would write her reminiscences of the wartime years in her book *In and Out of the*

Last Meeting of Lee and Jackson by Everett B. D. Farino Julio. Julio was a native of Louisiana and painted this famous scene after the war. For health reasons he came to Bartow County, Georgia, and was a guest at Spring Bank where he taught art in the private school owned by the Howard sisters. He died at Spring Bank and is buried nearby in the family cemetery.

Lines, published in 1904 at her own expense by selling acreage from Spring Bank. Fanny died in 1907.[33]

By the 1970s, the house at Spring Bank was vacant, the Howard family no longer the owners. On 1 February 1975, the house burned. A few years later the site and acreage that once belonged to the Howards was purchased by a timber company. In 2002, public interest in setting aside certain areas in rapidly urbanizing Georgia as "green space," supplied the money needed for Bartow County to purchase 38 acres at Spring Bank, inclusive of the Howard family cemetery and house site. Today under the personal supervision of a retired and dedicated university professor, and with the support of county labor and equipment, the history and natural resources at Spring Bank are being protected and cared for as they should be.

THE BATTLE AT CASSVILLE

On 19 May, Johnston's Confederate army seemed poised to strike a decisive blow upon the XX and XXIII Corps of Sherman's army near Cassville. Hooker's XX army corps, the vanguard of the Army of the Cumberland, was several miles east of Kingston marching on a road running directly to Cassville by way of Colonel Hawkins Price's house. The XXIII Army Corps was approaching Cassville from the northeast by way of the road from Mosteller's Mill and Spring Place.[34] Neither Federal corps knew that Hood's and Polk's armies were in nearby Cassville. Sherman had assumed wrongly that the two corps had remained with Hardee's Confederates in the retreat along the railroad from Adairsville to Kingston. It seemed for once the rebels would have numerical parity in battle. The plan was for Hardee's large corps to delay Sherman's main army (McPherson's and the majority of Thomas's army) east of Cassville long enough to enable Hood's and Polk's Confederates to win a stunning victory. Johnston's order to attack was worded in such a manner as to compliment soldierly character, inspire confidence in the opportunity for victory just ahead, and invoke the Almighty's blessings: "Soldiers of the Army of Tennessee, you have displayed the highest quality of the soldier—firmness in combat, patience under toil…. Your communications are secured. You will now turn and march to meet his advancing columns…. I lead you to battle. We may confidently trust that the Almighty Father will reward the patriot's toils and bless the patriot's banners."[35]

The plan of battle was for Polk to attack the Federals north of town near the women's college, while Hood hooked eastward in such a way as to strike the northern army in the flank while their attention was fixed on Polk. Johnston's order to attack was greeted enthusiastically by his soldiers. The disappointment from two weeks of retreat could now be replaced by a decisive blow at the invading army. What happened in the next few minutes on the Cassville battlefield that day would be hotly debated for years to come.

As planned, Polk began his approach to join battle. Hood had no sooner begun his flanking movement

The marker erected by the WPA on the site of the Cassville county courthouse Sherman ordered burned in November 1864.

2. Colonel Hawkins Price house near Cassville served as General Hooker's headquarters on 19 May 1864. Wilbur Kurtz took this photograph in the 1950s. The house has since been torn down and the site marked by a state historical marker. The original Kurtz photo is in the Kurtz Collection in the Atlanta History Center.

when he stopped it, claiming enemy infantry was eastward to his right flank.[36] This threw the timing of the whole Confederate attack maneuver into complete disarray. Johnston was inclined to doubt Hood's information, but decided on further reflection he must either act defensively or retreat. The decision to forego the attack and return to the defensive came as a great disappoint to many soldiers in the ranks of the Confederate army. The confusion generated by the quick reversal from attack to defense is registered in the diary of Lieutenant T. B. Mackall. After commenting on the instructions to change the line, Mackall noted that:

> Generals Johnston and…Polk [rode] on high hill overlooking town and back from original line. New line marked out, and troops rapidly formed on it and along a ridge. Late in afternoon considerably skirmishing and artillery, enemy's skirmishers occupied town. At one time confusion [during the withdrawal from the hills north of town]; wagons, artillery and cavalry hasten back; noise, dust, and heat. Disorder checked; wagons made to halt. Consternation of citizens; many flee, leaving all; some take away few effects; some remain between the lines.[37]

The new line meant abandoning the town and dropping back to a ridge running generally north and south, facing west overlooking the village, with Hood's corps anchored near the Posey House (just east of the town cemetery), Polk's corps on Hood's left, extending southward along the ridge facing west toward town, and Hardee's corps, entrenching from Polk's left, defending the main road from Kingston, extending across the railroad, with its left on a hill near the Foster House.[38] Here the 63rd Georgia saw action again.

On 19 May, the 63rd Georgia of Mercer's brigade had been advanced to support the skirmish line near the Foster House. Withdrawing from near encirclement in the nick of time, they experienced several casualties; among the dead was Legare Hill, son of Joshua Hill, a former US congressman from Madison, Georgia. Two companions "took up the lifeless body, conveyed it to a little cottage, pinned his name on his jacket and

left him there. Although this was done in full view of the Federal skirmishers, not a shot was fired until the two men had rejoined their
comrades. The Federals later took the body of young Hill, buried it, and
marked the grave by a headboard.[39] Later, during the siege of Atlanta, the
father, a past personal friend of General Sherman's brother US Senator

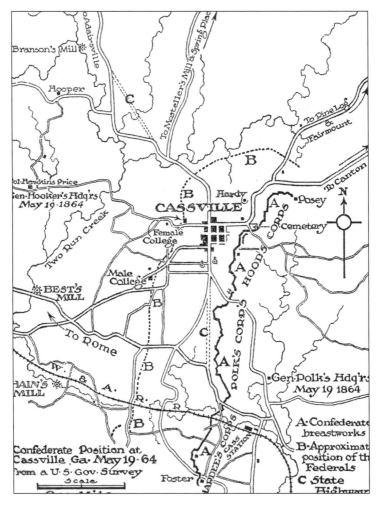

Kurtz map of Cassville showing roads and troop positions. Most often reproduced of the Kurtz
Cassville battlefield maps, it features the approximate location of the Confederate defense lines on
the east side of town. Note Hardee's lines cross the railroad and are anchored near the Foster
House.

John Sherman, asked the general's permission to return to Cassville to recover the body of his son. Sherman approved the request and in addition granted him permission to go by rail to the rear, carrying a note to the commanding officer, General John E. Smith, at Cartersville, requiring him "to furnish him escort and an ambulance for the purpose."[40]

This new line of defense placed the town of Cassville between the battle lines allowing Federal skirmishers the opportunity to occupy the village. Later, Jenkins Lloyd Jones, a private in the 6th Wisconsin Battery wrote his impressions of the village: "A very pretty country town hid away among the hills. A large college used as general hospital by the rebs here. Ascended to the observatory, had a splendid view. A large library filled with books going to waste."[41]

Withdrawal to a defensive position on the ridge east and south of Cassville now produced new complaints from Johnston's commanders. Hood and Polk felt their alignment would be vulnerable to Federal artillery and therefore difficult to defend. Hardee, on less favorable ground, felt certain of his ability to defend his position. He felt it could be held against any foreseeable attack. He was overruled at a council of war at Polk's headquarters at the McKelvey House that night. With two of his three corps commanders uncertain, Johnston felt he had no choice but to retreat. At 1:00 A.M. on 19 May, the Confederate army abandoned the ridge east of Cassville and headed south toward the river.

By afternoon of 20 May, the army had passed through Cartersville and was beyond the Etowah River, with supplies in hand and bridges burned behind them.[42] Within three weeks, Sherman had become master of the entire region between the Etowah River and Chattanooga.

THE BUILDING
AND BURNING OF CASSVILLE

By the third week of May, the village of Cassville was in the jetsam of battle. Following the Confederate army's withdrawal south of the Etowah River, a few citizens returned to town hopeful of resuming their lives reasonably undisturbed. This was not to be. Plagued throughout the summer and fall by raids from renegade bands of "scouts" (deserters from both armies) who preyed on civilians, attacked isolated units of the Federal army, and sabotaged the railroad, life in Cassville was found to be anything but peaceful. In truth it was quite chancy—a near perfect sea of anarchy. Despite Sherman's best efforts to capture these bandits, they found safety in their hideouts in the hills east of Cassville. A frustrated and vengeful Sherman ordered the entire town burned in November 1864. The town deserved better.

Cassville had its beginning in the 1830s during the Indian removal. Two early trading and military routes, the Alabama and Tennessee roads, gave access to the region; the site was considered picturesque and suitable for a sizeable town. It was surveyed for that purpose by state surveyors in 1832. The plan of survey called for: " Streets 40 feet wide bordered on each side by ten feet reserved for sidewalks ran north and south and [these] were crossed at right angles by others of similar width. The blocks formed were 210 feet square or one acre in area. The block in the center of town was reserved for the courthouse and the blocks surrounding this were surveyed into "business lots" 30 feet wide by 105 feet in depth."[43]

The town prospered from the first. The courthouse and new brick homes and houses of business, complete with sidewalks of brick, gave the town early on a look of urbanity; an impression certainly in keeping for a deserving political seat of the affluent new county of Cass.

Community leadership came from a mix of lawyers, doctors, and educators. Through their efforts two colleges were chartered by the state legislature in 1853; the Cassville Female Institute, soon to feature a brick building on a hill north of town, and the Cherokee Baptist College for men located nearer the village. To insure an appropriate moral atmosphere for this fledgling academic community, the legislature gave the town commissioners authority to control "spirituous liquors within the corporate limits of the town."[44] Cassville soon earned a reputation as a hard place to buy a drink. Students boarding in the village should certainly now be safe from these immoral influences. Registration fees and small endowments were depended on to meet the financial needs in both colleges. The curriculum in each school included a sampling of "Natural Philosophy, Chemistry, Algebra, Geometry, Botany, Latin and Moral Philosophy."[45] The student body numbered between 75 and 100 enrollees at each college depending on the year examined.

The town of Cassville prospered culturally in the 1850s as a result of these college activities. Sometimes graduation events would last an entire week, attracting considerable crowds of parents and friends to hear the formal discourses required of all graduates. Cassville as a county seat and a cultural center was indeed doing well by 1860. What was missing was the railroad.

The Western and Atlantic bypassed Cassville 2 miles south of town. During the railroad construction twenty years earlier, efforts had been made by the town fathers to persuade the state legislature to authorize the route directly through Cassville. Instead, because of the probability of a more costly construction due to the character of the topography encountered in a direct route to Adairsville, the state decided to bypass Cassville in favor of a longer but less rugged trace westward, via Kingston to Adairsville. After the war, for this reason and because of the expense of rebuilding war-torn Cassville, Cartersville replaced Cassville as the county seat. The absence of rail transportation, and the village's wartime destruction would prove to be the twin heralds of Cassville's fate—a town now vanished.[46]

The fires that proved so fateful for Cassville began on 12 October 1864 at the Baptist College. The college buildings of the male school were

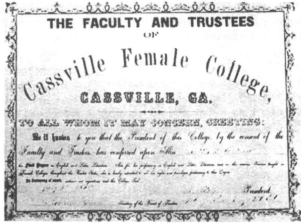

Cassville Female College and diploma,. Courtesy of the Etowah Valley Historical Society.

burned in reprisal for the murder of some Federal soldiers nearby on the night before by "raiders." On 5 November, the entire town was set to the torch. Sherman's orders were that "not a house, except the churches, should be left within the limits of the corporation." J. L. Milhollin, a fourteen-year-old, could never forget the afternoon his home was burned by the 5th Ohio Cavalry. He recalled the near panic of his mother, how he and his brothers and sisters helped take the planks covering their father's recent grave, and how they used these and quilts to create a makeshift tent attached to the cemetery fence as shelter for the family on that cold November night. The next day they moved their few household effects salvaged from the fire to an abandoned slave cabin some few miles away. The experience was still a vivid memory to Milhollin when interviewed nearly three-quarters of a century later.[47]

Frances Elizabeth "Lizzie" Gaines remembered the sacking of Cassville earlier by Federal soldiers immediately after the withdrawal of the Confederate army on 19 May:

> They had lost no time, after entering town, in ransacking and plundering every house, from cellar to garret. Many of the citizens, in the panic, had left all they possessed, expecting to be able to return as soon as the fight was over. No closet, drawer, nook or corner escaped their search. They took the most valuable articles and sent them home as trophies to their friends. Some of us who remained did not even find a change of clothing or one morsel of provisions—they had torn sheets, pillow cases, counterpanes, dresses, and everything of the kind into strings, broke crockery and cooking utensils, destroyed furniture, took what provisions they wanted, and if there was any left, messed it up in such a manner that it could not be eaten. For instance, they would mix meal, flour, soap, molasses, lard, sugar, preserves, etc., together so as to render it unfit for use.[48]

Lizzie Gaines also remembered the afternoon in November the town was burned:

> On the 5th of November Col. Keith of the 5th Ohio Regiment came with about three hundred cavalrymen and two or three pieces of artillery, to burn the place. He only gave us twenty minutes to get our things out. They offered us no assistance. Said they had orders to that effect. We were so frightened we scarcely knew what to do first.... They commenced firing the place between 2 and 3 o'clock [p.m.]. All our tears and prayers availed us nothing. We begged to hearts of stone. In a short while the Public Square was one vast sheet of flames. It soon spread all over town, and in a short time nothing was left but the smoky ruins and chimneys.[49]

Today, Cassville is a small working-man's village, rebuilt in a modest fashion after the war with little to show of its grand past. The two churches and a private house spared by Sherman, are identified by historical markers, and the site where the courthouse stood is marked by a

Cassville Cemetery commemorative plaque.

stone monument containing a metal plaque erected by the WPA in the 1930s. On a street leading east, one can visit wartime Cassville's cemetery and view Dr. Hardy's house nearby. Then, by traveling south out of town one will see, on the left, the battle ridge upon which Hood, Polk, and Hardee entrenched in 1864, and a closer inspection finds the earthworks still plainly visible. A short distance further along the drive south from town, on the right, is a grove of trees near the street. Here is the WPA pocket park with monument commemorating the "Battle of Cassville." Other then these few reminders, there is little evidence today of the story of wartime Cassville. Landmarks like the ruined brick buildings on College Hill have long since fallen victim to a four-lane highway and other "improvements." Only the churches and the Hardy house (east of town) survive as witnesses to old pre-war Cassville. Perhaps we must wait for the miracle of a restoration renaissance in Cassville generated by some energetic group of history-minded people such as those that stepped forward recently at Spring Bank. In 2003, the restoration of the historic past at Cassville awaits a preservation wake-up call.

Several Confederate soldiers were buried in Cassville Cemetery after having died in the nearby military hospital. In the confusion of war, names were not recorded or records were lost so most graves are unmarked. Several Confederate veterans who died after the war also buried in this cemetery.

10

CIVILIAN HARDSHIPS
IN THE PATH OF ARMIES

For Sherman, the retreat of the Confederate army across the Etowah River on 20 May was yet another instance of an escape by a foe in a frustrating series of similar experiences since Dalton to trap the rebel army. Sherman expected to corner this army, forcing it to fight despite its disadvantage in numbers; a helpless foe trapped by Sherman's perfect choice of time and place and then, of course, quickly destroyed and thus bringing this whole military matter of the campaign to a proper close. The Confederates, however, seemed always to escape the noose.

Sherman's anxieties and frustrations were further compounded by the ever-lengthening railroad line of supply on which he so depended. Each daily advance of his army increased the size of the sabotage target— each mile closer to Atlanta meant a mile further from his base of supplies in Chattanooga and Nashville, and of course, a mile more of vital supply line to defend. More soldiers would have to be detached to garrison duty at key positions along the railroad to guard the line leaving his fighting army ever smaller the closer it got to Atlanta. Either he must snag that rebel army soon or reinforcements must be found.[50] Most exasperatingly of all, with Confederate supply centered in Atlanta, the time required for replenishing the needs for the Confederate opponent decreased in proportion as his multiplied.

And protecting his supply life line was not Sherman's only concern. On the march, the slow-moving Army of the Cumberland was a continuous exasperation to him—"too quick to entrench at every small alarm," it needed constant prodding. In a mid-summer correspondence with General Grant, Sherman complained that his chief source of trouble was with the "dreadfully slow" Cumberland Army. "I came out without tents and ordered all to do likewise, yet Thomas has a headquarters camp on the style of Halleck at Corinth; every aide and orderly with a wall-tent, and a baggage train big enough for a division."[51] But many complained that Sherman violated the spirit of his own orders by providing himself with non-military food and housing whenever opportunity offered. His personal pack train was a marvel to see of food supplies, cooking ware, and an assortment of "Mutt and Jeff" mismatched cooks, providing all as they passed with an amusing parade of unmilitary looking contraptions and people:

> He had a sort of pack-mule train...a motley throng of mules and darkies, loaded down with mess-pans, camp-kettles, and all sorts of noisy implements...which followed closely after his staff and orderlies, like a harlequin escort. Every time his grotesque cavalcade passed a column of troops, it was greeted with derisive comments, and such chaff as only veteran soldiers know how to indulge in. As Sherman came in sight of his deployed lines [at Adairsville], he turned into a large, open field, with all his followers. They had hardly gone their length, when a volley of grape or canister came ripping across the ground, and rattled like hailstones on the side of a large barn just behind them. With one impulse, the whole procession turned tail and stampeded madly to the rear...the tin pans rattling as loudly as the shot on the barn, and [were] seen no more till next morning.[52]

Sherman spent the night at "Tom Town," General Thomas's headquarters camp for supper and rest.

For Sherman, never a patient man, traveling through a rugged country following poor maps and worse roads, and inhabited by a generally hostile population, the experience was one of mounting irritation with each passing mile. Still, Sherman managed to officially maintain the pretense of civilized rules of war. Unlike the March to the Sea later that year, the progress of the Atlanta Campaign would be characterized by some effort by leaders on both sides to limit the destruction to private property and to take steps to reduce men terrorizing of civilians caught in the path of war. The wholesale destruction of the villages along the railroad would come later (in November) when Sherman removed the tracks, and effectively razed the region of all settlements along the line of the railroad from Atlanta to Calhoun before departing on his march to the sea.[53]

Despite the spasmodic work during the summer by a few leaders on both sides, the renegade element from both armies made humanitarian efforts difficult to maintain during the campaign. Sherman, burdened with the anxieties over an over-extended railroad line of supply, soon lost any concern he might have had for humanitarianism and the rights of private property ownership. His charity eroded proportionate to the frequency of acts of sabotage on his rail line. On 23 June, in a general order, Sherman declared the use of torpedoes (land mines) placed under the rails to blow up passing trains, was "just plain malicious." To put a stop to the practice, he ordered therefore, that when mines were found in the possession of the enemy: "You may cause them to be put on the ground and tested by wagon-loads of prisoners, or, if need be, citizens implicated in their use. In like manner, if a torpedo is suspected on any part of the [rail]road, order the point to be tested by a car-load of prisoners, or citizens implicated, drawn by a long rope. Of course an enemy cannot complain of his own traps."[54]

At one point in the summer, Sherman required all civilians living within 3 miles of the railroad be removed. Still, for the most part, the traditional rules of civilized warfare regarding the treatment of civilians and their property remained the official policy in both armies until after the capture of Atlanta.

During the summer, several officers in Sherman's army and in the Confederate commands registered official dismay at the rampant destruction they witnessed daily. General John Schofield, commander of Sherman's Army of the Ohio on one occasion singled out the 124th Indiana Regiment for a special reprimand. Men of this regiment, he said, had been left to guard the trains of the army; they had instead been found guilty of "violence and depredation on the defenseless inhabitants of the country through which we are passing." Schofield went on to declare that the commander of the regiment would be severely reprimanded, and that he was determined to "enforce discipline and suppress disorderly and disgraceful conduct by every means possible.[55]

The conduct of renegades from the Confederate army was just as bad. Major General Joe Wheeler advised his cavalry command on 31 May that:

> The families of officers and soldiers of this command, as well as other citizens, are frequently robbed of their horses, provisions, and grain by mounted men, who roam over the country falsely representing themselves as scouts detached from this command, and falsely representing that they have authority from these headquarters to impress said articles… In cases where citizens are trespassed upon they should first learn what troops are committing the trespass, and then report that fact to the nearest officer, who will immediately see that proper steps are taken to secure justice to the citizen and the Government.[56]

On 23 May, Milo S. Hascall, the commander of the 2nd Division of the Army of the Ohio commented regarding what he considered a "terrible state of things that exists in different parts of the grand army under Major General Sherman, so far as the wanton destruction of private property and works of art is concerned." Hascall went on to say that he had witnessed daily as "many as half a dozen houses and barns on fire at a time." He said further that this state of affairs is "enough to disgrace and render worthy of defeat any army in the universe." Hascall declared that he had "no desire to serve with an army where the fundamental principles of civilized warfare are so shockingly violated at every step in our progress."[57] Still, Hascall seems to have adjusted reasonably well to Sherman's style of warfare; he remained with the army throughout the summer as a division commander during the siege of Atlanta, and participated capably in the final battles near Jonesboro.

Two weeks after Sherman's departure from Atlanta, the Georgia governor Joseph Brown received a report detailing the destruction wrought upon Atlanta:

> The car shed, the depots, machine shops, foundries, rolling mills, merchant mills, arsenals, laboratory, armory, etc., were all burned
>
> In the angle between Hunter Street, commencing at the City Hall, running east, and McDonough Street [Capitol Avenue], running south, all houses were destroyed. The jail and calaboose were burned. All business houses, except those on Alabama Street, commencing with the Gate City Hotel [corner of Pryor], running east to Lloyd Street [Central Avenue], were burned. All the hotels, except the Gate City were burned. By referring to my map, you will find about 400 houses standing [in a 4800-foot radius from present-day Underground Atlanta]. ...[Y]ou will see by this estimate the enemy have destroyed 3200 houses. Refer to the exterior of the circle, and you will discover this is more than half a mile to the city limits, in every direction, which was thickly populated, to say nothing of the houses beyond, and you will see that the enemy have destroyed from four to five thousand homes. Two-thirds of the shade trees in the Park and city, and of the timber in the suburbs have been destroyed. The suburbs present to the eye one vast naked, ruined, deserted camp.[58]

11

THE PLANTATION BELT
ALONG THE ETOWAH

---·•·---

There is one region in the path of these armies that summer that remained unscarred—the Etowah River valley. From Cartersville to Rome we see today the grand homes of a planter class. The river valley offered rich soil and the Western and Atlantic and the Rome railroads provided convenient transportation.[59] These people came from Virginia and South Carolina, as well as from Georgia. It was here that North Georgia's only antebellum cotton plantation belt came to exist. Why these houses were spared the torch is difficult to learn—perhaps it had something to do with the presence of Schofield's Army of the Ohio. That army was the first to arrive and one of the last to leave the valley. The *Official Records* and the regimental histories tell us that Schofield and many of his commanders objected to the wanton destruction of property and unnecessary harassment of civilians. Whatever the explanation, the Etowah River valley offers today an inventory of magnificent antebellum houses—private homes occupied in many instances today by the descendants of those who built them.

Atop a hill overlooking the Etowah River valley near Kingston is "The Bricks." Built in 1846 by Benjamin Reynolds of Virginia, this two story stately building with four freestanding Doric columns, was constructed of handmade bricks manufactured near the building site. Reynolds had come to the state a few years earlier attracted by the gold rush in North

Georgia. Prospecting unsuccessfully near Villa Rica (in Carroll County), he bought land in Bartow County and built The Bricks—returning to the more familiar life of a planter, although the cash crop here would be cotton rather than tobacco as had been the case in Virginia.

The house features a hanging balcony with a "spindle balustrade, topped with a decorative wheat-sheaf railing."[60] There are twelve large rooms, with a detached kitchen connected to the house by way of a covered breezeway. The Reynolds' house was used by the Federals as a field hospital during summer 1864, and is identified on military maps and mentioned several times in the *Official Records*. The house is a private home today not open to the public.

Down the road about 5 miles is "Valley View." Tradition has it hat General John Schofield spent some time here in May 1864, and that several soldier autographs were left on the interior walls of the house—one of these remains in a closet on the second floor: "Newton Westfall, Co. C 4th Cav., Sept 7th 1864." Colonel J. C. Sproull and his family had migrated from Abbeville, South Carolina, in 1839 and built Valley View on a high knoll overlooking a bend in the Etowah River. A daughter, Rebecca Sproull, kept a diary during wartime, recording life at Valley View between 1861 and 1864, how the family abandoned the house when cannon was heard at nearby Cassville, and how when they returned later that year they found the keyboard and strings of their valuable piano "ripped out and the case used as a trough in which to feed the horses."[61] The case was salvaged and the piano repaired.

The setting at Valley View is near perfect. Driving from Cartersville along the Euharlee Road, one turns in at stone gate posts and travels a half-mile-long driveway to the house. The house features freestanding Ionic columns across the front and a portion of two sides of the building. The building is constructed of brick. The hanging balcony across the front is missing its original decorative iron balustrade. It is said that Federal troops in 1864 removed the iron and melted it into cannonballs.[62] Today, Valley View remains a private home occupied by direct descendents of the Sproull family.

On New Year's day 1911, "Shelman Heights" burned to the ground. The story of Cecelia Stovall Shelman's brief romantic encounter with

(top) The Bricks in Kingston. This handsome antebellum brick home was built by Benjamin Reynolds in 1846. This house was a military landmark in 1864, serving as a hospital for Confederate and Union armies. This house is identified on Sherman's maps of the area. The Bricks is a private home today. (bottom left) This antebellum mansion along the Etowah River is believed to be the Ayers House indicated on Sherman's map. (bottom right) Oakdale, the John A. Johnson House at 573 Reynolds Bend Rd., is clearly marked on Sherman's map and is privately owned today.

Sherman continues to be told today. She had met William Tecumseh Sherman at the West Point Military Academy in 1836 while visiting her brother, Marcellus Stovall. Stovall and Sherman were cadet roommates. Sherman is said to have been romantically "smitten" by this dark-eyed beauty from Augusta, Georgia, but she turned him away telling him his

(top) Valley View as it appears today. Beautifully maintained by Bob and Mary Norton, direct descendents of the original owners, Valley View is a private home and only rarely on public tour. (bottom) Walnut Grove, former home of General Young, is occasionally on public tour and is owned by direct descendents of General Young.

eyes were "so cold and cruel" and that she pitied any man who was his foe: "Ah, how you would crush an enemy."[63] Sherman had replied that even if she were his enemy, he "would love and protect [her]."

In 1864, he was leading his great Federal army past Shelman Heights, the home of Cecelia Stovall Shelman. Some of his men were preparing to burn the house when Sherman learned that it was Cecelia's house. Upon hearing this, Sherman ordered the house protected and left a written note for Cecelia with a servant. "You once said that I would crush an enemy and that you pitied my foe. Do you recall my reply? Although many years have passed, my answer is the same. I would ever shield and protect you. That I have done. Forgive all else. I am only a soldier."[64] The note was a treasured family heirloom in the years following the war. Cecelia Stovall Shelman died at Shelman Heights in 1904; she was said to be "witty and charming and the center of attention to the end of her days."[65]

"Walnut Grove" was the home of the family of Confederate General Pierce Manning Butler Young, believed to have been the youngest major general North or South. The house was built in 1840. This two-story

Shelman Heights, home of Cecelia Stoval Shelman, Sherman's West Point "sweetheart."

building of bricks has a portico supported by square columns; the long gallery of smaller porch posts is at the back of the house.[66] Walnut trees were cut nearby for use as interior paneling and stairway, and some trees were carved into furniture. The grounds around the house retain a formal beauty of English boxwoods and centuries-old walnut trees. Young resigned from West Point in 1861. A dashing Southern soldier, he was seriously wounded twice, and on one occasion, when warned that the charge he was about to lead was certain suicide his reply was "I'll be a major general or in hell in half an hour." After the war, Young served as United States congressman from Georgia, and was appointed consul general to Russia by Grover Cleveland.[67] Walnut Grove is located near Cartersville and is privately owned.

These four antebellum house sites along the Etowah River are representative of the many interesting homes between Cartersville and Rome. And there always seems to be a story that goes with each. Today, these houses are private residences open to the public only on special occasions.

12

CROSSING THE ETOWAH INTO THE WILDERNESS

The crossing of the Etowah by retreating Confederates on 20 May seems to have been seen as a campaign milepost for both armies. Sherman would describe the Etowah River in correspondence as his "Rubicon"; no turning back. For Joe Johnston's Confederates, disappointment, another mile closer to Atlanta without a decisive battle; the opportunity at Cassville seemingly wasted. As for the Federals, many hoped the two-day pause at the river would become a welcome break from constant marching, and perhaps even an opportunity for some much needed rest. It was used instead as time for the preparation of required food, and for wagon-loading equipment and supplies for an extended foray away from the railroad into the Georgia wilderness. Sherman was planning a bold twenty-day cross-country sortie as the next phase in his campaign. Expecting to bypass the rebel army entrenched in the unassailable rugged Allatoona hills south of the Etowah River he would, with rapid marches via Dallas, outflank the foe, thus threatening the Confederate army's vital rail supply to Atlanta and forcing them to give battle on his terms. Two problems existed with this plan: first, by abandoning his railroad and depending entirely on supplies furnished by mule-drawn wagons and gambling on good weather for an extended period, he was seriously diminishing his advantages over his foe, a foe who remained for the time being ensconced on the railroad and comfortably supplied. Second, the rebel army was not likely to wait passively in the Allatoona hills. Learning within twenty-four hours of Sherman's maneuver, Johnston's Confederates marched rapidly to block the Federal progress at New Hope Church and Dallas. The battles for the "Hell Hole" were about to take place.

In these few days of respite at the river, Confederate soldiers on picket duty at the Etowah River had time to reflect on the technical and supply advantages demonstrated by their opponents over the past several weeks. The speed and efficiency with which the Yanks repaired the railroad and bridges was a marvel to witness. Much of the credit went to Colonel William W. Wright, a civil engineer in the Federal army. Wright was the chief construction supervisor commanding a corps of 2000 combat engineers whose task it was to maintain bridge and road repair on the rail line. One source describes Wright's practice of taking ordinary wooden bridges of the railroad reconstructing with a standard pattern of truss using interchangeable parts, and keeping prepared timbers in stock at safe points in the rear.[68] Many of these timbers were prefabricated

The Western & Atlantic Railroad crossed the Etowah River on five stone piers during the Civil War (Here, the other three are obscured by foliage.). The bridge was abandoned in 1946 when the railroad crossing was relocated downstream to allow for the construction of the Allatoona Dam.

trusses manufactured in Nashville to fit the width of the rivers and carried by railroad flatcar to Georgia when needed. Many river bridges burned by the Confederates in their retreat would be back in service within twenty-four to forty-eight hours. A story goes that a Confederate soldier witnessing these repairs remarked that since the Yanks repaired bridges about as fast as the Rebs could destroy them, perhaps they should have blown up the railroad tunnel at Tunnel Hill. According to local legend, his dejected companion responded that such a tactic would probably not have worked since Sherman "likely carried a spare tunnel with him."

Sophisticated construction engineering skills were not the only technical advantage enjoyed by Sherman. Instantaneous communication between him and principal subordinates and military superiors was maintained by telegraph: "A light train of wagons carrying wires and insulators moved with the headquarters; the forest trees were used as poles; an operator with his instrument accompanied each army commander, who could converse directly with the central station and with General Sherman himself."[69] The telegraph was supplemented on the frontlines with the usual encrypted flag signals, or by mounted courier. The Federal army seemed ready in every way for a formidable military excursion into the Georgia wilderness. The Federal mishaps in this wilderness in the next few days would cause the battleground ever after to be called the "Hell Hole."

13

THE BATTLE
AT NEW HOPE CHURCH

—◆—

We were marching down a beautiful shady country road in a southerly direction parallel with the Chattanooga and Atlanta railroad and a few miles to the west of it. The Federal army under Sherman was still to the west of us, at least, that was our understanding. We came to the cross-roads at the church, were ordered to halt, stack arms, and rest, with no thought of being in battle soon. We were lounging around resting not more than thirty minutes when we heard a few guns fire to the west of us, and about a mile distance.[70]

By noon on 25 May 1864, the battle at New Hope Church was near.[71] On 22 May, Sherman had issued the march orders in preparation for crossing the Etowah River and for the movement south toward Dallas. He instructed the divisions of George H. Thomas's Army of the Cumberland (centered at Kingston) to cross the river and move on parallel roads southward through Euharlee and Stilesboro to Dallas. Jefferson C. Davis's division of John Palmer's XIV army corps, being at Rome, was to march via Van Wert (Rockmart) directly to Dallas. The remainder of McPherson's Army of the Tennessee was to march to Dallas via Van Wert keeping to the right of the Army of the Cumberland. John

Schofield's Army of the Ohio was to cross the river east of Euharlee and then take march routes southward to Burnt Hickory (now Huntsville), staying to the east of Thomas, and taking a position northeast of Dallas on the Cumberland Army's left flank.

Crossing the Etowah River on this hot and dusty mid-May day would be the first challenge for the Federal soldiers. Private Ira Owens of Company C of the 74th Ohio remembered how

> Some of the boys prepared to wade, by taking off their shoes and pantaloons.... Others went right in, without taking off anything. I did so myself. When about half way across, where the water was nearly breast deep and running very swift, I thought I would go ahead of some who were ahead of me, when I stumbled and fell, losing my gun, and getting a complete wetting, filling my haversack with water and soaking my hardtack. I recovered my gun which would not have been of much use, should we have an occasion to use it.[72]

On 23 May, Confederate General Joseph E. Johnston became aware that Sherman was south of the Etowah River and marching rapidly toward Dallas. From his headquarters at the Moore House, just south of the river, near the railroad cut at Allatoona, Johnston ordered his corps commanders to proceed immediately to Dallas along the Acworth-Dallas Road to intercept the Federal forces before they could gain control of the ridge-line roads near Dallas that led to Marietta and Atlanta. From his location near Allatoona, Johnston's use of the Acworth road to Dallas would give him the advantage of the inside angle to Sherman's line of march and therefore a shorter mile march-distance to cover to reach a position blocking the Federal movement.

By 24 May, Hardee's Confederates were just east of Dallas facing west in position to check the Federal advance toward Marietta, and Hood's corps marching on the Acworth-Dallas Road, was rapidly approaching the New Hope Church crossroads 3 miles from Hardee's right. Polk's corps, Johnston's intended center, was delayed after taking a southward

The Moore House near the railroad cut at Allatoona Pass. This was General J. E. Johnston's headquarters just prior to the battles near New Hope Church. Today the Mooney family own the
house as a family residence.

detour west by way of the Dr. James Peters house near Mars Hill Church,
seeking a less crowded alternate route to New Hope via Lost Mountain.
Because of the greater march distance, Polk's infantry on 25 May was on
a road leading to Dallas south of the New Hope Church crossroads near
Hood's position rather than linked to Hardee's right at Dallas 3 miles
west as had been intended. On 25 May (the day of the battle at New Hope
Church) this left a dangerous 3-mile gap in the Confederate defense line
between New Hope and Dallas. During the night of the 25th Johnston
corrected the problem by shifting troops from the three Confederate
corps to seal the gap between Hood's and Hardee's flanks.

In 1864, the field of battle at New Hope Church crossroads resem-
bled the wilderness battlefields in Virginia. Poor roads and dense thickets
favored the defender because concerted control of assault movements

under such conditions was virtually impossible. A participant described the topography near these crossroads:

> In front of New Hope Church was a valley wooded along the road, but with open fields a little further to the north, and the stream, which is a branch of Pumpkin Vine Creek, flows northwesterly at that place, parallel to Hood's front. The banks sloped easily on either side, and were some fifty feet in height. The whole of Johnston's line was admirably chosen for defense, occupying as it did a series of ridges covered with wood on their summits, but having open valleys in front, over which attacking forces must advance without shelter. It covered the roads leading from Dallas to Atlanta, to Marietta, and to Ackworth [sic], as well as those passing near New Hope Church in the same directions.[73]

The Stegal House in Emerson GA was General William Hardee's military headquarters for several days in mid-May 1864. The house was designated an historical structure in 2002 by the community of Emerson and is today restored and owned by the city.

The route taken to New Hope Church by the Federal XX Army Corps in 1864 is today as then, called the Cartersville Road. A portion of this road leading from Owens' Mill in 1864, no longer in use today, begins at the mill site on Pumpkin Vine Creek. From Owens Mill the trace of this now abandoned road runs generally eastward along a ridge, passing by the Hawkins House (See atlas map.) located a little more than a mile east of the mill and reaching a connecting point with the modern Cartersville Road a half mile or so west of the present-day Mt. Zion Church. This road, today as then, continues eastward along the ridge, bordered by deep ravines on either side that radiate from the road in generally southwest and northeasterly directions. Just past Mt. Zion Church, the road begins a long crescent-shaped curve to the right, a down-slope, gradually changing direction to almost due south and traveling a distance of a little more than a mile, then rising gradually to the crossroads at New Hope Church. About 200 yards west of the crossroads, near where the road presently passes the eastern edge of the New Hope Cemetery, the terrain on the west side of the road is laced with deep ravines. Like extended fingers from an open palm, these ravines radiate from the roadside in a confusion of intersecting, narrow, maze-like gullies with sharply-sloped banks covered with an almost impenetrable mix of scrub sweet gum, pine thickets, briers, and vines. Evolving from narrow, interlacing steep ravines at the road, they fall away, flatten out, and become a meadow a few hundred yards west of the 1864 Confederate battle line on the hill at the cemetery. Over this difficult ground, midst this confusion of thickets and ravines, Federal General Joseph Hooker's XX army corps would blunder into deadly combat on 25 May, a field of battle that the Federals would long remembered as the "Hell Hole" at New Hope Church.

Making their way into this region by 7:00 A.M., the three divisions of Hooker's XX army corps were marching south on roughly parallel roads seeking to unite with McPherson's Army of the Tennessee just north and east of Dallas. Geary's 2nd Division was the first to reach the burning bridge at Pumpkin Vine Creek near Owens' Mill. While extinguishing the flames they were fired upon by nearby Confederate cavalry—the first shots in the battle at New Hope Church. With General Hooker present and approving, Geary ordered one of his brigades forward to engage the

Confederate skirmishers. Opposing Geary's 5000-man division was Confederate Colonel Bushrod Jones of Hood's corps leading an under-manned infantry brigade consisting of the 32nd and 58th Alabama supported by some attached cavalry and sharpshooters, beleaguered with repeated orders from Hood to delay the Federal advance as long as pos-sible, Jones did the best he could. His entire force including cavalry, numbered less than 300 men, yet he received oral and written orders from Hood to "press vigorously forward [to] make the enemy develop their strength, and then to hold the position."[74] Jones fought stubbornly, even recklessly, withdrawing slowly toward New Hope Church, retreating only when nearly surrounded. Although outnumbered more than five to one, Jones led his regiments in charge after charge against the advancing brigade of Geary's division. On one occasion the "charge was made with [such] spirit and vigor, [that it] broke the regiment in [his] front,"[75] but soon, so heavily outnumbered, Jones was driven back. At one point the scrappy Confederates were able to take a strong position on a knoll where they managed to make a stand for fifteen or twenty minutes.[76] On a high hill—near present-day Mt. Zion Church—on the Cartersville Road about a mile west of New Hope crossroads, Hooker halted Geary's division to await reinforcements, convinced by the resistance from Jones's small band that a significant portion of Hood's corps must lie ahead. This post-poned the attack more than an hour. The effect of this delay allowed the Confederates more time to prepare, entirely forfeited the element of sur-prise, thus diminishing the Federal advantage in numbers, and used up precious daylight. Bushrod Jones's spirited resistance had paid off. Hooker was certain that two other divisions would surely be needed to assist Geary.

Backtracking from their march routes west of Owens Mill and delayed by wagon and troop-jams on the worse-than-bad roads through swampy woods, the afternoon was well spent before Alpheus Williams's and Daniel Butterfield's divisions took position near Geary's. The tactical formation selected by Hooker was a column of brigades; an ill-chosen formation that achieved control advantage for the greater disadvantage of overly exposed flanks on a narrow battle front. The result was that the three Federal divisions forfeited a five-to-one numerical advantage by using a formation that gave a tactical front of only 300 yards. Again and again each division attacked by brigade front, with the several brigades in each division relieving each other by passing lines. Fifteen thousand Federal infantry were stopped cold by one 3000-man Confederate division—and a portion of this division was not entrenched out of respect for the dead in the cemetery they occupied.[77] In the middle of the battle a thunderstorm broke over the combatants, followed by a night-long cold, heavy rain. In addition to these natural elements, there was a continuous rattle and volleying of musketry, heard nearly to Burnt Hickory more than 20 miles away. In the darkness, as fresh attacking Federal columns heard these sounds of heavy combat, they stumbled blindly through woods. General Geary's division bore the brunt of the action:

> By 5 p.m. both [divisions] had come up and massed. Williams on my right and Butterfield on my left and rear. Each division was quickly formed for attack in columns by brigades. Williams leading, Butterfield next, my division as a reserve, and the corps advanced upon the enemy. The discharges of canister and shell from the enemy were heavier than in any other battle of the campaign in which my command were engaged. The night was intensely dark, and a very heavy thunder-storm, with cold, pelting rain, added to the gloom. It was therefore impossible to form a regular line with the troops, and all the dispositions of them we could make was by the fitful flashes of lightning. Breast-works were thrown up as fast as possible during the night, and the dead and wounded were all cared for before morning.[78]

For the Confederates at New Hope Church the battle on 25 May would be remembered as a victory by a single division over assailants greatly outnumbering them. This single division was commanded by General Alexander P. Stewart of Hood's corps. Stewart's division, marching en route to Dallas to assist Hardee in blocking Sherman's flanking move, happened to arrive at the New Hope Church crossroads near noon on 25 May in perfect position to block any Federal move on

Rick Reeves's painting *Holding the Position* shows a portion of the Confederate defensive line at New Hope Church on 25 May. Specifically, the painting probably depicts that part of Stewart's defense near the New Hope cemetery where entrenchments were not used out of respect for the existing graveyard.

that point. Upon hearing the sound of distant firing from the direction of Owens' Mill, Stewart was ordered by Hood to deploy his division to defend the crossroads. Brigadier General Alpheus Baker's brigade was placed on the right of the Cartersville Road facing northwest, Major General Henry D. Clayton's brigade prolonging the line westward astride the road, and Brigadier General Marcellus A. Stovall's brigade in position in the church cemetery where it remained unentrenched throughout the battle out of respect for the graves of the dead. Stewart's infantry was effectively supported by Major J. Wesley Eldridge's battalion of artillery.

Eldridge's sixteen-gun battalion was led by captains Thomas J. Stanford, McDonald Oliver and Charles F. Fenner and their batteries; all guns were "well posted" and prepared to do "great execution."[79] In the action that followed, these guns fired more than 1,500 rounds. All gunners battled heroically, but none matched the gun crew of the three Bridgen brothers in Fenner's Louisiana Battery: "The oldest was the rammer. He was shot down, and the second brother took his place. In a short time he was shot down, and the third took his place [and] shortly he was shot."[80] An eyewitness from a nearby vantage point wrote later of the battle scene and the work of Confederate artillery:

> It was while we were standing in the road [at the church crossroads] before moving to the front that we were in full view of both lines while the battle was raging. The grounds were open for a distance of two hundred yards from the road, and then were thickly timbered, through which the enemy advanced, and they halted at the edge of the opening. Our artillery cut down the timber and did great service on that occasion. The enemy was prevented from bringing up artillery on account of the dense forest through which they came. Both lines remained entrenched that night.[81]

Stewart's division remained in position throughout the New Hope Church battle needing no reinforcements. Many soldiers were inspired by the personal leadership of General Stewart who calmly rode his roan horse along the battle line seemingly unconcerned for his own safety. While engaged in these reckless saunters, "talking to his men and urging them to do their duty," Stewart would remember later:

> As I rode along, the fire of the skirmishers grew quite hot, and as I passed the post occupied by my son, Lieut. R.C. Stewart, he called out to me: "Now father, you know you promised mother that you would not expose yourself to-day." At once the quick-witted men took up the remark, and I passed to the end of the line amid their laughing cries of, "Now father, you know you promised mother that you would not expose yourself today."[82]

For the Federal participant it was a day of anxiety, frustration, and despair. A soldier witnessing the hopelessness of Hooker's attack commented afterward on the futility of the battle; how with Hood's Corp behind breastworks it would require desperate fighting to dislodge them. And how the assaulting columns moved up with a rush to the very breastworks again and again, heroically challenging the deadly gunfire and how they died by the scores and hundreds on those earthworks. He described the whole experience as "simply slaughter." He felt that "Sherman had blood to spare, and that Hooker poured it out that day in the dark forest as though human life had no value. The steady sheet of flame pouring over the logs scorched and withered the blue lines until they had to draw away from it."[83]

Because of the storm, night descended early on the fighting at New Hope bringing yet more misery with the darkness. For Hooker's men, caught in the confusion of these dense thickets and ravines, darkness proved to be "intensely dark." Sergeant Rice C. Bull of the 123rd New York Infantry of Williams' Division remembered the death premonition of his friend Sergeant James Cummings just before the battle at New Hope. Bull described Cummings as a fine soldier, a physical giant of over 6 feet and well educated. Cummings was usually cheerful, but that day he seemed sad and melancholy. Cummings had confided in him that he had had a lingering feeling over several days that he would not survive his next battle. Bull reminded his friend that we all had such thoughts but that they never came true. A few hours later, Cummings and Bull were lying side by side in the rain and mud in the "Hell Hole" near the Confederate battle line at the cemetery. It was about 9:00 P.M.: "and the battle was winding down though bullets were still whistling overhead. The artillery had stopped firing and the night was black as 'an inkwell.' Suddenly Cummings rose slowly to his feet, placing the butt of his rifle on the ground and stood quietly facing the enemy."[84] When Sergeant Bull cautioned his friend that he was recklessly exposing himself, he answered that he did not think "there was anymore danger in standing here than lying in the mud. I have had enough of that." Cummings remained standing, leaning on his gun less than a minute, when Bull "[h]eard a metallic sound, as though one had taken a hammer and hit a tree with it. Cumming's gun dropped from his hands and he and his gun struck the ground at the same time. A bullet had found its mark in his forehead, passing through his brain. We carried him back to the field hospital where he died before morning. In his death our company lost its best soldier."[85]

Breastworks were constructed in the darkness throughout the night aided by the glow of lightning flashes. In his diary, Major Stephen Pierson of the 33rd New Jersey Regiment (Geary's division) remembered how the storm of shot, shell, shrapnel, and minie balls burst upon them as they neared the Confederate line at the cemetery. Pierson goes on to describe how limbs of trees broken by Confederate artillery shells fell upon them and how "all about us was the shriek of shot and shell and vicious song of the minie bullet, accompanied too often by the sickening thud which told that it had found its mark in the body of a man in blue." The 33rd New Jersey and the other regiments of Geary's third brigade worked in the darkness "like beavers," digging with hands and bayonets, throwing up dirt to create the beginning of a defensive trench:

> Then a few shovels came up; down in the ravine the pioneers [combat engineers] cut down trees, logs were rolled up and put on top of the little ridge of earth. Short sticks 3 to 4 inches thick were placed under the logs and through this crevice we could safely see to shoot. I remember very well the fierce thunderstorm that came up that evening, but the lightning in the skies and the thunder in the heavens seemed but little incidents compared with the flash of the guns and the roar of artillery, which, at frequent intervals, through that night and every night for a week, broke out, as one side or the other thought they detected signs of an advance against them.[86]

By daylight on 26 May General Geary could see that his entrenchments ran along a low ridge confronting the Confederate position on the slightly higher ridge at the cemetery. Geary's line ran perpendicular to the Cartersville Road; some 80 yards from the rebel position on the left flank and 300 yards where his right linked with Williams's left down in the meadow west of the road. Geary described his situation that dawn:

Around us in all directions were thick woods. The [Cartersville] road to New Hope Church passed through my lines occupied by Candy's Brigade, the flank of which, on the left of the road, was not in connection with any other troops. At this point near the road my lines were closest to those opposing us, and sharpshooters from Candy's brigade were posted so as to command a battery [Fenner's?] in his front, preventing the enemy from working his guns, excepting now and then to deliver an occasional shot.[87]

The battle of New Hope Church was now essentially over. From the morning of 26 May until Sherman abandoned the position near the cemetery and crossroads on 4 June, the fighting here settled into a daily routine of sniping and trench warfare. Locked in a deadly tactical embrace with opponents in some instances separated by only a few yards, no effort was made by either side to risk certain destruction with a foolhardy assault against such impregnable defenses. Still, with the battle lines in such close proximity, the heavy sniper fire produced substantial

New Hope Church Confederate Cemetery has remains from many of the New Hope battlefield casualties, but several are Confederate veterans who died years after the war.

casualties each day until the New Hope Church crossroads battlefield was abandoned by both armies on 4 June.

This bloody experience at the church crossroads on 25 May had cost the three divisions of Hooker's XX Army Corps more than 1,600 casualties—almost 700 killed in action, with several missing and likely dead. Adding to these numbers, the several hundred casualties experienced by the supporting IV and XXIII Army Corps in the same vicinity on 25 and 26 May, Sherman's army must surely have suffered at least 2,000 killed, wounded, and missing at New Hope Church. This "Hell Hole" experience, with a similar assortment of dismal thickets and ravines and dismal tactics was repeated two days later by the IV, XIV, and XXIII Army Corps 3 miles east—a place called Pickett's Mill.

Confederate belt buckle: Twisted in half between the "C" and the "S" on 25 May 1864 at New Hope Church; the "C" left on the battlefield until 1964, the "S" recovered 300 yards away in 1998—the two halve united today. Displayed in 2006 in a private museum in Kennesaw.

14

PICKETT'S MILL AND THE PRESERVATION OF THE SITE

A mbrose Bierce in *Ambrose Bierce's Civil War* said, "There is a class of events, which by their very nature, and despite any intrinsic interest that they may possess, are foredoomed to oblivion." So it was believed by many who witnessed the Battle of Pickett's Mill on 27 May 1864, in Paulding County, Georgia.

The Federals on 25 May had managed the New Hope Church battle badly; mistakes and errors of judgment were responsible for many of their almost 2,000 casualties. With lessons surely learned, Sherman's army resumed the flanking tactics that had been so successful during the first twenty days of May. This flanking assignment went to IV Corps commander Major General Oliver O. Howard with General Thomas J. Wood's division spearheading the way. Wood's immediate task was to locate the extent of the Confederate entrenchments eastward and to attack them at the appropriate point.

The morning of 27 May found Wood's division making its way over bad or non-existent roads attempting to locate the elusive flank of the Confederate line. By 3:00 P.M., they had reached what they considered the desired point of attack near Pickett's grist mill on Pumpkin Vine Creek. The Federal forces numbered some 14,000 men. Colonel William H. Gibson's 1st Brigade took up position in the sun near a large field less than 400 yards from freshly dug Confederate entrenchments. Brigadier

General William B. Hazen's 2nd Brigade formed on a rise of ground a few hundred yards downstream from the mill. In reserve was Frederick Knefler's 3rd Brigade. To Hazen's left was a division from the XIV Corps commanded by Brigadier General Richard W. Johnson. Part of this division extended across the creek. Gibson's right was to be protected by a brigade from the XXIII Corps commanded by Brigadier General N. C. McLean. During the course of the battle McLean's brigade would fail to support the attack as directed and would later retire without orders "to replenish its supplies." The principal burden for the attack at Pickett's Mill would fall on the IV Corps with expected support from the XIV and XXIII Corps.

These Federal forces faced Major General Patrick R. Cleburne's elite Confederate division. Positioned on the left along Cleburne's line was Lucius Polk's and Daniel Govan's veteran brigades. Extending from Govan's right overlooking a deep ravine was the Texas brigade commanded by Hiram B. Granbury. On his right, continuing down the ridge toward the mill, was Mark P. Lowery's brigade arriving during the course of the battle and doing the best it could to protect itself with whatever log barricades opportunity afforded. To the right-front of Granbury's position, down near the mill, was the Widow Pickett's farmhouse. (Earlier that day, the Texans had explored the house, finding it empty. Before fleeing, the Pickett's had attempted to store their household goods; the Texans discovering a featherbed and other domestic articles in an old well.[88] It would be these four brigades of Cleburne's division that would bear the brunt of battle that day at Pickett's Mill.

As it is today, the battlefield at Pickett's Mill in 1864 was covered with dense thickets and cut by steep ravines. A major portion of the Confederate position lay concealed in a dense covering of underbrush. In General Cleburne's after-action report, he leaves us a graphic description of the topography: "Between the spur and the principal ridge was a deep ravine the side of which next to Granbury was very steep, with occasional benches of rock up to a line within thirty or forty yards of Granbury's Texans, where it flattened into a natural glacis. This glacis was well covered with...trees and in most places with thick undergrowth. Here was the brunt of the battle."[89]

The Federals took up an assault formation in columns of regiments. "We will put in Hazen and see what success he has," commented the commander of the IV Corps. At approximately 5:00 P.M. Hazen's brigade stepped off. A few moments later, Gibson followed with his brigade but experienced artillery fire from his right "which caused him to recoil" and he was granted permission to halt and refuse his right so as to protect his brigade thus leaving Hazen's 3,000 men to do the job alone. Gibson's delay of forty-five minutes was fatal to the success of the attack. Wheeler's Confederate cavalry (dismounted, 800 strong, and astride the creek near the mill) was able to fire into Hazen's left flank while at the same time disrupting the advance of General Scribner's brigade of Johnson's division (XIV Corps) advancing along the creek, thus throwing the Federal timing off on that key part of the battlefield.

As Hazen's men advanced they lost unit integrity because of the dense underbrush. As they emerged from the ravine they were slaughtered by Granbury's right and Lowery's left. In his *Civil War*, Ambrose Bierce, an eyewitness, called this the "dead line" because in the space between the ravine and Granbury nothing got past that point without being shot. One battalion of Hazen's brigade drifted to the left in such a way as to come out of the ravine on Lowery's right flank near the mill at the creek. Here the Federals had their only real opportunity for success that day but were ultimately frustrated by the delay of the XIV Corps and by the quick response of a Confederate counterattack to the threat on Lowery's flank. The ultimate cause of failure that day for the Federals was piecemeal waste of three good infantry brigades, and the one-hour delay of Scribner's brigade (XIV Corps) by Wheeler's dismounted Confederate cavalry along the creek, leaving Hazen's and Gibson's flanks "hanging in the air." Adding insult to what had already been an injurous day for the Federals was a surprise bayonet charge by Granbury's Texans at 10:00 P.M. capturing several hundred wounded and frightened Federal soldiers in the ravine. The next day there were more than 700 Federal dead buried in mass graves near Granbury's lines. According to the most reliable count, the Confederates lost 85 killed and 363 wounded, while the Federals lost more than 1,600 casualties in the Battle of Pickett's Mill—a badly managed battle ignored by Sherman in his memoirs. It seems that no lessons

Kurtz painting of the wartime mill house at Pickett's Mill. The building was destroyed during the battle but was rebuilt after the war and operated as a grist mill by the Pickett's family for several years. Mr. Kurtz drew this sketch from descriptions from eyewitnesses who had seen the original building. Today, only the foundation footings remain at the site—cared for by the state-owned Pickett's Mill Battlefield staff.

in judgment and tactics had been learned by the Federals from the battle two days before in the "Hell Hole" at New Hope Church.[90]

After the war, the Pickett's Mill battlefield rested in private ownership. Paulding County remained a rural area. Small family farms dotted the landscape. Morton R. McInvale in his book *The Battle of Pickett's Mill—"Foredoomed to Oblivion,"* described the families that inhabited Paulding County after the war as "…substantially the same stock, from the same families, and with the same traditions as their prewar counterparts." This was the way it stayed until about the turn of the century. According to McInvale's research using deed and plat books to trace land ownership, "much of the land in Paulding County around the site of the Pickett's Mill battlefield passed from private ownership into the hands of real estate, insurance, or timber companies. The land reflected the change. No longer was it primarily agricultural in usage with cleared fields and pastures. Instead, it began to grow up in timber."

In McInvale's study, he traces every transaction involving the land on which the battle was fought. The most significant transactions began in August 1932. According to McInvale's study of county land records, "The Prudential Insurance Company sold to a certain C.E. McMichen Lots 977, 1040, 1041, the west half of Lot 1042, and one acre in the southern part of Lot 1050." McInvale also lists another purchase made by W. V. and C. E. McMichen on 1 October 1951. They bought 300 acres that included lots 969, 971, 974, three-fourths of lot 975, the west part of 972 and 973, and 18 acres of lot 901. The McMichen brothers then sold 200 acres to the North Georgia Timberland Company on 16 August 1952. This

Pickett's Mill battlefield relics found by Ralph Righton and Phil Secrist in the 1950's and 1960's near the sites of a field military hospital and the battle ravine.

land consisted of lots 970, 971, 974, and three-fourths of lot 975, end lots 972 and 973, and 18 acres of lot 901.

This was not the end of North Georgia Timberland Company's purchases. They bought 54 acres from J. F. Marchment on 9 June 1952. This land consisted of "all of Lot 976, the southwest quarter of 969, and four acres in the southwest corner of Lot 975." North Georgia Timberland Company now owned 395 acres on the site of the Pickett's Mill battlefield—a small detail of which they were totally ignorant. In practice, they would not have cared less if they had known. Timber and profit was their single focus. The company held this land for the next two decades.

In 1957, armed only with the knowledge from Confederate General Cleburne's report in the *Official Records*, Secrist set out to find the location of this long-forgotten battle site. Two others, Beverly Dubose and Atlanta historian and artist Wilbur Kurtz had preceded him several years in a successful quest to locate this unmarked field of battle. Their success was a close-kept secret because of Dubose's battlefield relic hunting interests. They left only a single metal marker (anchored in a concrete base) along the ridge road to the mill site indicating this location as the battlefield of Pickett's Mill. Locals in the vicinity depended primarily on oral history passed down by family and knew only that a Civil War battle had been fought there.

After reading the Cleburne description of the battlefield terrain, the Secrist was able to find the ravine where the Union troops were massacred by the partially entrenched Confederate troops. Over the next few months he was able to match terrain and official story with supporting artifact evidence. Over the next several years, Secrist explored the battlefield recording trench locations and key physical features on the battle site. In May 1971, *Civil War Times Illustrated* published Secrist's article on the Battle of Pickett's Mill, "Scenes of Awful Carnage." This was the first in a series of rapid events that culminated a year later in the preservation of the battle site of Pickett's Mill.

In summer 1971, it was learned that Georgia Kraft (formerly North Georgia Timberland Company) had decided to sell certain Paulding County holdings. Ernie Stone, a professor at Southern Tech College near Atlanta with an interest in real estate investment, brought this information to his faculty colleague Phil Secrist who recognized the historic site on Stone's land plat as that of Pickett's Mill. Secrist made a phone call to Cobb County attorney Fred Bentley. Bentley, history minded and a prominent member of the community, soon put together a group of five investors willing to take the risks of purchasing the Georgia Kraft property. In addition to Secrist, Stone, and Bentley, Jim Ayers of Home Transportation Services and Alan Sellars of Oxford Manufacturing Company pooled their money and bought the battlefield. Using the name Property Management Services, Inc., of Cobb County, the group purchased eight separate tracts from Georgia Kraft on 24 September 1971. Simultaneously, Property Management Services bought the Paulding County holdings of Piedmont Southern Life Insurance

Company. On 10 December 1971, Beneficial Investment Company (formerly Property Management Services of Cobb County) was deeded the bulk of its purchases from Georgia Kraft. Beneficial had purchased lots 969, 970, 971, 974, 975, 976, 977, 978, 1040, 1041, 1050, half of 1042, and portions of 901, 972, and 973. The total land involved was 467.76 acres. According to Billy Townsend, the chief historian for the Department of Natural Resources, Beneficial paid approximately $1,200 an acre for the property when they bought it from Georgia Kraft and Piedmont Southern Life Insurance Company. During the next two years Beneficial Investment Company held the land.

Whether by design or by luck, there was a big push by the Federal government to preserve our past and money had been allocated to the states to find such projects. In Georgia then-governor Jimmy Carter created a Heritage Commission to study, evaluate, and rank sites based on certain criteria. The "criteria" was known as the Site Selection Plan and was being developed with Pickett's Mill as the working model. Over the next few years the Heritage Commission collected and compiled its data and issued a report in 1974 entitled "The Final Report of the Georgia Heritage Commission." In this report the Pickett's Mill site was not ranked because by this time it had been purchased by the state.

According to Billy Townsend, as the Heritage Commission was compiling its report, Georgia's Department of Natural Resources was working in conjunction with the Heritage Commission to establish the criteria to rank the different sites. The criteria detailed in the Site Selection Plan included nine areas. Historical integrity was first, followed by "best of kind, historical deficiency, site integrity, ease of management, developmental potential, geographical distribution of sites, endangeredness, and lastly appropriate resources."

The primary criterion was historical integrity. The Site Selection Plan defines historical integrity as "a measure of the extent to which the original components of the feature have been retained." Components consist of things such as original location, fabric, appearance, and environment. "The extent to which these four components are present in a feature help to determine it value in comparison with other features." The Site Selection Plan also defines what is meant by each of these components.

"Original location is identifiable through geographical coordinates, addresses, landmarks, and tangible remains." The existence of original fabric refers to the material of which the feature was originally constructed. Original appearance is defined as "any alteration, addition, and topography should be considered when evaluating the original appearance of the feature." And lastly, environment. When this criterion is considered, concern is for any changes that may have taken place in the area surrounding the historic feature.

The historical integrity of the Pickett's Mill battle site can be summed up in a quote that appeared in a feasibility study conducted by the Environmental Planning and Engineering, Inc. This study was presented on 15 December 1972, to the Georgia Department of Natural Resources. The report stated the "Pickett's Mill has all the factors needed to provide a historical site as the existing site conditions are very near the actual conditions at the time of the battle. Combining these three areas [New Hope Church, Dallas Battle Line, Pickett's Mill] would create a unique experience for the people of Georgia and their visitors." The report concluded redundantly that "the consultant recommends Pickett's Mill battlefield."

With the state satisfied and the site purchased, development at the site had to be addressed. According to warranty deeds, the state of Georgia purchased the 467.76 acres owned by Beneficial Investment Company on 28 July 1973. According to Billy Townsend, the state paid $3,000 per acre, for a grand total of $1,403,280. On 12 November 1974, the state bought an additional 82.545 acres from Georgia Kraft Company for an undisclosed amount of money. On 10 December 1974, the state bought 79.56 acres from the Alephi Land Investment Ltd., also for an undisclosed price. This land consisted of lots 1112, 1113, and 1114. These purchases gave the state a grand total of 629.806 acres at Pickett's Mill.

As the plans for the park grew so did its need for additional land. For example, access to the park was expected to be a problem so additional property had to be purchased to insure a proper route in and out of the park. As adjacent lands became available the state made offers to purchase. On 14 August 1979, the state bought 116.8436 acres for $128,527 from Mrs. Oma Bickers. This same lady (according to Townsend) had gotten up at a town meeting and told state representatives that "she wanted a state park next to her like she wanted a hole in the head." Her land consisted of lots 1043, 1046, and 1047. This was an especially important acquisition because it included part of the mill site. The final parcels of battlefield property were acquired by the state in 1981 making a grand total of more than 700 acres and giving Pickett's Mill the distinction of being the only state or federally owned Civil War battlefield in the United State preserved in its entirety.

Politics also had its role in the preservation of the Pickett's Mill battle site. At the time the land acquisition events were taking place a young state representative named Tom Murphy became speaker of the House. According to Townsend, Murphy's Confederate great grandfather fought at Pickett's Mill. In a letter from Murphy to George Bagby (then director of the Department of Natural Resources) dated 11 August 1973, Murphy requested an update on the progress of the Pickett's Mill preservation. He made a point to let Bagby know that he (Murphy) has "been very interested in this park and was at least partly responsible for putting one-half million dollars in the budget for the purchase of the land. I would like to see some results at a very, very early date." He goes on to say that "If I do not hear from you in the next few days, I will come by your office to view such plans as have been made and will expect to see some progress having been made at that time."[91]

Bagby quickly fired off memos to his subordinates to gather information on what progress had been made. He emphasized the importance of a timely delivery of this information by attaching a photocopy of Speaker Murphy's letter. The staff's responses were immediate. One Robin Jackson sent a reply to Bagby stating that "work has been scheduled to begin on this park September 1, 1973. Four months have been allotted to this project giving us a completion date of January 1, 1974. Still, much work had to be done...an access road from the nearest public road had to be cut and paved, and a visitor's center and museum created to mention just two."[92] The park was not officially dedicated until 24 May 1990.

What plainly emerges from the Pickett's Mill preservation story is the necessity of several important components: (1) Private initiative repre-

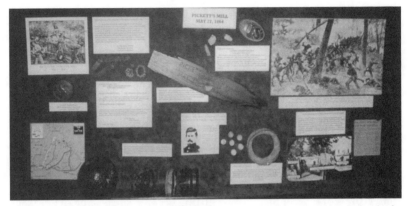

The Pickett's Mill field recovery exhibit displays numerous relics from the site, including the far right shell base—the first relic the author discovered at the site.

senting a concern for historical preservation and blended with some promise of profit to justify the financial risks. (2) Political savvy as in the case of Tom Murphy who while wanting the project to go forward realized that he needed political cover should the project fail. He used two front men, George Bagby and State Representative Charlie Watts. Their job was to "push through the needs of this project." What they asked for they got. Funding for any part of the project was never denied. And (3), since Pickett's Mill is a historical site, there needed to be an agreement among historians on the merits of the project. Syd Kerksis, a former Federal employee and an avid and successful Civil War relic collector, and Jeff Dean a staff employee with the Department of Natural Resources who served several years as the on-site custodian of Pickett's Mill and became well informed concerning the battle, joined the author (a college history teacher) in agreeing what constituted the major events of the battle, and that the site deserved preservation.

When the pieces of the story are thus presented, we are tempted to see a pattern or model emerge. While it may be pleasing to hope that the Pickett's Mill story can be duplicated with a possibility of protecting other worthy sites in the future, we must remember that only two of the components discussed here can be readily replicated: (1) an historically deserving site, and (2) private initiative. In the Pickett's Mill story a large sum of money became available at the very time a large tract of land (Pickett's Mill battlefield) was offered for sale—and political allies appeared early and in the right places. Such components are more difficult to replicate. Perhaps the story of the preservation of the Pickett's Mill battle site can best be characterized as a happy coincidence of opportunity and personal initiative. Still, such an achievement is inspiring and the results certainly enduring.[93]

15

THE BATTLE OF DALLAS

By 25 May, a substantial portion of McPherson's Army of the Tennessee was approaching the village of Dallas, Georgia, having marched on several roads via Van Wert (Rockmart) and Burnt Hickory (Huntsville). The XV Army Corps moved quickly through the town southeastward along the Villa Rica Road. Taking defensive positions on rugged, wooded hills about a mile south of town, their line facing and parallel to the road and in close proximity to the Confederate battle line (near the present location of Paulding County High School), the XV Army Corps awaited the expected arrival of the supporting XVI Army Corps. For most of its length, Logan's three divisions of his XV Army Corps occupied the high ground along the east side of the Villa Rica Road. This line of defense faced east, except for Colonel Reuben Williams's 1st Brigade of W. M. Harrow's 4th Division. Williams's brigade, linked on the left to Walcutt's 2nd Brigade at the Villa Rica Road, extended westward at a right angle several hundred yards along a low ridge beginning near the present-day intersection of Verlon Aiken and Villa Rica roads. The left of Williams's brigade connected with Charles C. Walcutt's 2nd Brigade (4th Division) at the Villa Rica Road forming a right angle in a defensive alignment. Reinforced by two companies of the 6th Iowa, Williams's brigade thus became the extreme right flank of McPherson's battle line at Dallas. It was here at this link of two brigades on the Villa Rica Road on the south side of Dallas, that fighting became especially heavy on 27 and 28 May 1864.

The close proximity of the Confederate and Federal battle lines here on the Villa Rica road made early contact certain as both armies constantly jockeyed for space along their skirmish lines, resulting in a continuous escalation of contact between the contesting parties. By late

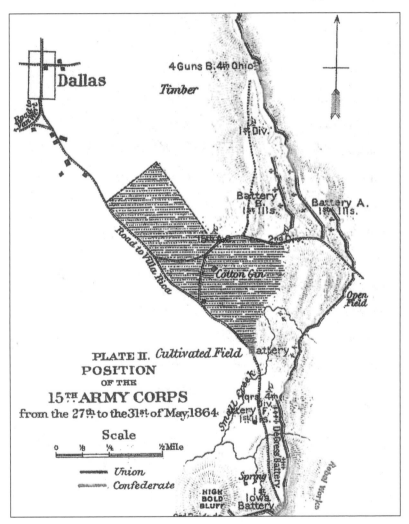

Sherman's map of the Dallas battlefield. The Confederate battle lines were a few hundred yards south along the ridge near the present location of Paulding County High School.

afternoon on 27 May, a division of Confederate infantry, partially concealed in their approach by a nearby wooded ravine, struck suddenly along the Villa Rica Road hitting the 1st and 2nd brigades of the 1st Division, causing considerable consternation. The attackers were forced to retreat after a half-hour's fight due to heavy rifle fire from the Federal line and an unexpected bayonet charge by three companies of the 6th Iowa Regiment. Corporal John W. Clemson of the 46th Ohio Infantry (Walcutt's Brigade) recalled later how his unit was within 120 paces of the Confederate works and, although surprised by the sudden onslaught by the rebels, his regiment held its ground: "our boys were armed with Spencer rifles…seven-shooters. After the battle, a rebel asked, 'say Yank, what kind of guns have you-all got over there? Wind 'em up on Saturday night and they run all week?'"[94] Later that night Clemson's unit was reinforced by Wilder's cavalry brigade, also equipped with Spencers. Wilder's brigade took a position east of the Aiken Road serving as a screen against a possible surprise attack by Confederates from that direction. Following the fight on 27 May, Captain Francis DeGress's six-gun battery of 20-pounders was placed on the high ground along the east side of the Villa Rica road in advance of the 2nd Brigade, for the purpose of dueling with the Confederate artillery some 1000 yards further east.

Confederate pressure increased along the Villa Rica Road throughout 28 May. The night before, Sherman had ordered McPherson to begin disengaging his forces at Dallas as the first step in a planned withdrawal via New Hope Church to the railroad. This was in keeping with Sherman's decision to shift the entire Federal army eastward to rail at Acworth. Harrow's 4th Division on the Villa Rica Road was to initiate the withdrawal movement on 28 May with an artillery barrage at 4:00 P.M. to test the alertness of the Confederates—the reply was instantaneous:

> Quicker than thought, almost, the enemy attacked us in force, and with the greatest vigor and determination. The skirmishers on the roads were quickly driven in. Three lines of the enemy could be distinctly seen rapidly advancing, but they were soon checked by a determined line. On the right bayonets were fixed to receive the column that was

advancing with such numbers and impetuosity that it seemed they must break through my weak line…. the enemy making repeated attempts to carry my position…; were repulsed after severe fighting of one hour and twenty minutes.[95]

The drama in this engagement included the capture by Confederates of three guns of the 1st Iowa Battery near the intersection of Villa Rica and Aiken roads in the first few minutes of the battle on 28 May. Colonel William Smyth, commanding the 2nd Brigade that day, described this action in his official report:

Three field pieces of the First Iowa Battery…in position outside of our breast-works, had been captured by the enemy. This we learned from the drivers, who were taking the battery horses to the rear after we were ordered to support the Sixth Iowa. Our coming to the support of the Sixth was so gratifying and encouraging to them that, with our assistance, they poured a fire into the enemy so rapid and effective that the enemy was compelled to relinquish the three cannon they had taken and retreated precipitately, the Sixth's boys went out and hauled back the cannon by hand.[96]

Walcutt's Brigade report lists 244 Confederate dead and wounded left on the battlefield in his front. The Confederates reported their loss as 300 casualties; Federals reported 379 casualties for themselves.

The action on the Villa Rica Road south of town on 28 May was only part of a greater battle that extended northward and westward beyond the XV Army Corps to include the front of the XVI Army Corps. Some of the heaviest fighting took place there. Here on the east side of town the Confederate Orphan Brigade of Kentucky (Bate's division) persisted in an attack long after it was hopeless. Misunderstanding the signal intended for the attack, and encouraged by some initial success in breaking the Federal defenses, the charge was an extremely gallant one: "As they ascended into our semi-circle position where we had a galling fire upon their front, right and left flanks, they came with heads bowed down and their hats pulled over their eyes as if to hide from inevitable death. They left 600 dead in the semi-circle."[97] Badly hurt in this death trap, the Orphan Brigade ceased to exist as a fighting unit. As one Federal commander commented: "The losses to [this] brigade was so great that the memory of the engagement as one most destructive of it, was treated as a cause of special sorrow by the Confederate officers and soldiers long after the war."[98]

The events in the battles near Dallas, and the New Hope Church and Pickett's Mill line, had no significant bearing on the outcome of the campaign, nor did they cause serious delay in Sherman's advance toward Atlanta. The Federal army simply shifted its line of supply back to the railroad on 4 June and the new focus became Kennesaw Mountain and Marietta, with the Chattahoochee River and Atlanta just beyond. Three lessons are learned by the two armies in their first thirty days of combat: (1) Dependable supply is by rail only; (2) entrenching will save lives, and (3) the Almighty knows no favorites and only He controls the weather. The weather would dictate the character of the military campaign for the next three weeks.

16

THE WAR YEARS IN ATLANTA

he battlefield was now at Atlanta's doorstep. By early June, the people in Atlanta were literally in the immediate backwash of battle—the front line was just across the Chattahoochee River in neighboring Cobb County. There in Cobb County, the battles for Atlanta would be fought for the better part of the next six weeks. The Almighty and His weather would take center stage for much of this time.

The sounds of battle had first reached Atlanta's residents around the middle of May. The fighting, they learned, was taking place more than 30 miles away in Paulding County in a small country hamlet named New Hope. They were told that Joe Johnston was firmly in control; that any day now he would turn on his antagonist and strike the blow that would free Georgia of the invader. But now, the citizens were reminded daily that they had practical problems that needed attention. Citizens traveling

A scene of downtown 1864 Atlanta by Wilbur Kurtz.

by wagon or carriage in Atlanta encountered deep holes in the streets due to the heavy traffic of military vehicles and overloaded civilian wagons, a situation compounded by an inadequate system of street maintenance. In February 1864, the city council took note of these conditions and moved that the necessary repairs be made prior to the coming of the spring rains.[99] The Fulton County Grand Jury expressed its dismay at the proliferation of slaughterhouses and mule yards on the western side of the city. In an effort to remedy this source of irritation, the grand jury brought indictments against a number of citizens who were accused of maintaining unsanitary pens on Whitehall and McDonough streets.[100] The grand jury also expressed concern for the growing number of idle and aggressive teenagers who loitered about the streets and who were suspected of frequenting houses of vice. The editor of an Atlanta daily newspaper felt sure that a group of boys whose ages ranged from ten to thirteen, whom he had chanced upon playing a card game called "seven-up" with Confederate paper money were thus practicing the tricks of the devil and perhaps were already hopelessly advanced in the race to damnation.[101] The grand jury suggested correction houses for these young incorrigibles, and admonished the law enforcement officials to do their duty. In a more constructive vein, the jury recommended that schools for the education of the poor of the city be established so as to occupy these young minds in a more positive fashion.[102] Wartime priorities, however, would intervene before such measures could be carried out.

Atlanta had a war scare two years before, on 12 April 1862. A group of twenty-two daring Yankee spies, a mixed crowd of military and civilian young men, all disguised as civilians, made their way to Marietta pretending an intention to enlist in the Confederate army. They were actually part of a larger plan. By stealing a locomotive and sabotaging the Western and Atlantic Railroad between Atlanta and Chattanooga, burning rail bridges and destroying the tracks, the raid was intended to prevent reinforcements from Atlanta reaching Chattanooga in time to save that city from capture by a Federal army striking from middle Tennessee. This daring raid was led by a Union spy named James J.

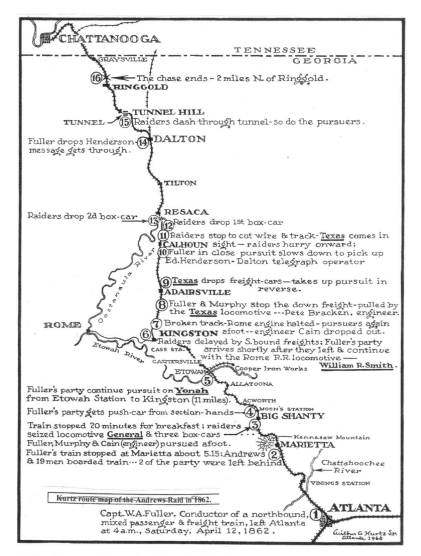

A Wilbur Kurtz map showing the flight of the ill-fated Andrews Raid.

Andrews; the Andrew's Raid became one of the great folklore stories of the Civil War.

The Andrew's Raid was doomed from the beginning. A heavy rain the day before soaked the bridges making the timbers less likely to burn.

The raiders had made their way in pairs from Tennessee to Marietta, Georgia. Here, they stayed the night of 11 April 1862 in the Kennesaw House, a trackside hotel, intending to catch the early morning northbound mixed freight/passenger train. The raiders, attired in civilian clothes, boarded the train shortly after 6:00 A.M., remaining in their seats a few minutes longer when other passengers disembarked at the Lacy House in Big Shanty for the usual twenty-minute breakfast stop. Taking command of the train when the locomotive engineer joined conductor William Fuller and passengers in the Lacy House for the usual breakfast, Andrews and his raiders headed north on their mission. Fuller, realizing to his dismay that the train was pulling away without him, gave pursuit on foot. What Walt Disney later called the "Great Locomotive Chase" was on its way.

Fuller, who became the Confederate hero in the story, was the personification of persistence from the beginning. Starting the pursuit on foot, he acquired in order, a railroad construction push car then a yard engine, enabling him to close the gap at Kingston in the 30-mile chase. Delayed by stops to cut the telegraph wire, remove rails, and frustrated in several futile attempts to burn the rain-soaked bridges, the raiders were further delayed by a forty-five-minute jam of south-bound rail traffic at Kingston. It seemed that Fuller was winning the race. Just north of Kingston however, more rails had again been removed, forcing him to abandon his second locomotive, and putting Fuller back in the race on foot. But persistence again paid off. In a few minutes, a south-bound freight pulled by the locomotive *Texas* was flagged down; the engineer was persuaded to back the train to nearby Adairsville, shunt his boxcars to a siding, and continue with Fuller in pursuit of the *General* and its raiders, at full steam, in *reverse*. The raiders, realizing at last that serious pursuit was gaining, and that stopping to remove rails and cutting telegraph wire was not improving their chances of escape (the mission of sabotage now entirely out of the question), they opened the throttle and focused only on escaping. The two locomotives raced at speeds of up to 60 mph, along fragile tracks and roadbed designed for safe speeds of 20 mph. Because of the overnight rains wetting the wood fuel, the raiders on the *General* were having trouble keeping their head of steam, causing the locomotive to slow down and finally coming to a stop just north of Ringgold. Here Andrews had no choice but to tell his men to make a break for it—every man for himself. The whole mission aborted, the men now scattered to the hills.

Within a week, all Andrews raiders were captured and imprisoned in Chattanooga. Eight were tried as spies in a Knoxville courtroom and all who were tried were sentenced to be hanged, Andrews included. Removed after the Knoxville trial back to the Chattanooga jail, Andrews and several of his followers escaped, but were rounded up a few days later. All twenty-two raiders were then transported to the Fulton County jail in Atlanta. Andrews was the first to hang, then the remaining seven of those convicted in the Knoxville court were hanged from a single scaffold a few days later. Frightened by this hard justice, the remaining prisoners staged another jail break. Making their way at night in pairs, one pair managed to escape by rafting down the Chattahoochee River to the Gulf, the remaining pairs by following the stars at night to their Union army units in middle Tennessee—several of them just in time to be captured again a few weeks later in the battle of Chickamauga. These Chickamauga unfortunates were returned to their jail cell in Atlanta to await trial and probable execution.

No more executions would take place. In a few months these daring men were exchanged as prisoners of war and were the first American soldiers to receive the newly created Congressional Medal of Honor. As a civilian, James J. Andrews was not entitled to the Medal, and thus the leader of the raiders was never so honored for his heroism.[103]

The Andrews raid and related events had kept the town of Atlanta at a fever pitch in the drama of the War. Now the year 1864 would find Atlantans embroiled in the tragic devastation of siege and battle from which there would be no relief and no escape.

THE FIRST BATTLES
IN COBB COUNTY IN 1864

By 1 June, the armies were shifting eastward from Pickett's Mill toward the railroad. Cobb County was now the center of military events in Georgia. On 3 June, Schofield advanced his second division across Allatoona Creek to the ridge just beyond, near the Foster House. Here in the extreme northwestern corner of Cobb County Schofield collided with entrenched Confederates on the crest of a hill at the intersection of two country wagon roads, Burnt Hickory and Acworth-Dallas. The grounds near the Foster house became the scene of heavy fighting. The men of Cox's 2nd Division, having dashed across the creek in the middle of a thunderstorm, began barricading themselves with logs and dirt and experienced heavy rifle fire and canister as darkness fell. Soon, with the rain continuing and the creek becoming a swollen torrent, the men realized that they were isolated from supporting divisions for the night. Despite these anxieties at the creek, and aware of the possibility of severe casualties should the nearby Confederates attack, the men of Cox's division passed the night without serious incident in this battle at Foster's Farm.

With Sherman's continuing shift to the east, by 3 June Federal cavalry had occupied Acworth and the hills overlooking the Etowah River. Now the reconstruction of the railroad bridge could get underway. On 11 June, the job was complete—the sound of a locomotive whistle south of the river approaching Acworth announced that Sherman's rail supply was back in business.

And the movement of great armies continued in a business-like fashion. By early June, McPherson's Army of the Tennessee was at Acworth, moving south along the railroad toward Big Shanty; Thomas's Army of the Cumberland was marching southward towards Marietta along the Stilesboro road in northwest Cobb County, and Schofield's Army of the Ohio was following the retreating Confederates along the Burnt Hickory road in the direction of Lost Mountain. The roads and fields in Cobb County had been transformed into a beehive of military activity.

The Confederate entrenchments recently abandoned in Paulding County ran east about a mile from Pickett's Mill along a commanding line of ridges, then nearly north along the Dallas-Acworth Road bordering the county line, reaching a point near the Foster House at the intersection of the Burnt Hickory road in Cobb County. Because of the continuing shift of Federal forces eastward toward the railroad, the Confederates had abandoned these entrenchments at Pickett's Mill and the Foster House on the night of 4 June, withdrawing eastward to construct a new 12-mile line of earthworks extending from Lost Mountain toward the railroad, past Kennesaw Mountain, to a ridge of hills just beyond named Brushy Mountain. Here for the next several weeks, along this series of hills and ridges in Cobb County, history would record the next battle chapter in the struggle for Atlanta.

Near the midway point on this new battle line was Pine Mountain, a solitary peak somewhat in advance of the principal Confederate defensives. At Pine Mountain on 14 June, Lieutenant General Leonidas Polk, the bishop/general, commander of the Confederate Army of Mississippi, would be killed by a Federal artillery shell.

Polk's headquarters had been at the George W. Hardage home on the Burnt Hickory Road some 3 miles southeast of Pine Mountain. Hardee had ordered Bate's division to entrench on Pine Mountain several days before. By 13 June, Thomas's Army of the Cumberland was approaching the mountain along Stilesboro Road and beginning to envelope Bate's isolated position. Johnston, concerned about the unprotected flanks of this division, called a meeting at the site for the purpose of discussing the danger with his senior commanders, Hardee and Polk. The artillery located on the hill near Bate's infantry was a four-gun battery of the legendary Washington Artillery of New Orleans. Down below in the valley, a mile away from Pine Mountain, Captain Peter Simonson's 5th Indiana Battery had found the range and an artillery duel between the two batteries was in progress when the three generals arrived. Attracted by this group of officers silhouetted on the crest of Pine Mountain, Simonson fired three rounds in quick succession, the third of which struck Polk, killing him instantly. The body was carried to Atlanta where a funeral ceremony was held at St. Luke's Episcopal Church, with the burial a few days later in Augusta. Although the loss of the sometimes controversial Polk would not greatly effect future Confederate military fortunes,[104] his death was a personal loss for friends of a virtuous man and a respected religious leader. General Johnston expressed these thoughts in a general order published on 15 June to the Army of Mississippi:

> Comrades, you are called to mourn your first captain, your oldest companion in arms. Lieutenant General Polk fell today at the outpost of this army, the army he raised and commanded, in all of whose trials he shared, to all of whose victories he contributed. In this distinguished leader we have lost the most courteous of gentlemen, the most gallant of soldiers. The Christian patriot soldier has neither lived nor died in vain. His example is before you; his mantle rests with you.[105]

Pine Mountain was abandoned by Bate's division in the predawn hours of 15 June.

The day of 15 June had been chosen by Sherman to test the Confederate defenses along the 12-mile Lost Mountain/Brushy Mountain line. Believing the length of the line too great for the Confederates to hold in strength, given the size of its army, Sherman ordered a reconnaissance in force at two points along this line. McPherson would attack at Brushy Mountain, a short distance east of the railroad near Noonday Creek,

The obelisk was erected in the early 1900s in a public ceremony to honor the fallen General Leonidas Polk. A nearby marker tells the story of the general's death on 14 June 1864. Just beyond the obelisk you can see a portion of the Washington Artillery fortifications; it was in these earthworks in the 1950s that this unexploded Hotchkiss artillery shell was recovered.

while Hooker's XX army corps would make a three-division attack in the day near Lost Mountain at Gilgal Church, extending eastward to a hill called Pine Knob. The three veteran divisions of Hardee's 25,000-man Confederate corps would be defending this line between the church and the knob. Butterfield, Williams, and Geary's divisions would be making the attack that day, with Geary's 5,000-man division of easterners[106] striking hardest at Pine Knob and taking the heaviest casualties for the day. For the 60th New York Infantry Regiment of Geary's division, 15 June would be an especially long day.

Geary's division, still healing from the "Hell Hole" at New Hope Church three weeks before, discarded their field packs in late afternoon near Pine Mountain and formed lines of battle facing due south, beginning the advance precisely at 5:00 P.M. Butterfield's division, three

The Dixon House on Acworth-Due West Road in west Cobb County. This house is on the battlefield of Gilgal church. The Dixon House was General Joseph Hooker's headquarters on 17 June — several correspondence from that site are in the *Official Records*. From as interview with Mrs. Clifton Lovinggod, the owner of the house in 1975, I learned that her father had purchased the house in 1919 "full of bullet and shell holes." She told me of an artillery shell that burst near the house during the battle. I later took pictures of the path of the shell fragment through several floor joists under the house! That damage remains today. (See chapter 29 for update.)

quarters of a mile to the west, began its advance at the same time along the Sandtown Road, past the Dixon House,[107] moving in the direction of Cleburne's Confederate division at Gilgal Church. Schofield's Army of the Ohio was to protect Butterfield's right by assaulting Lost Mountain, and Williams's division, considered in the first phase of the action the reserve for Geary, was expected to slip to the right during the course of the action in such a way as to link the two unconnected flanks of the divisions of Geary and Butterfield. Howard's IV army corps was to protect Geary's left by moving in conjunction southward toward the Confederate position.

Geary's assault path was laced with timbered ridges running generally northwest from the parent ridge occupied by the Confederates. Each of these secondary ridges and ravines was stubbornly defended. By the time the Federal infantry approached the main Confederate fortifications, darkness was approaching. General Geary described the fighting here as desperate:

> The enemy, driven with heavy loss into powerful entrenchments, on which they has bestowed a week's labor in preparation, and which in my front, they used eighteen pieces of artillery, fought from these works, knowing that if they were carried by us all to them was lost. In front of them the timber was slashed, and strong abatis, and also chevaux-de-frise of pointed stakes, had been formed. My troops, charging into the abatis, in some places within fifty yards of the guns, by dark had many of them silenced.[108]

The 29th Pennsylvania Regiment, joined by the 60th and 102nd New York regiments, constituted the first of the two assault lines in Colonel Barnum's 3rd Brigade's attack on the Confederate defenses that day.[109] An officer commanding that Pennsylvania unit described the experience of his unit advancing over hills "clear of standing timber and…evidently…prepared for defense. Their works not being seen, our line gallantly advanced, receiving a destructive volley of ball and canister from the enemy… it was thought impossible to storm their works. Accordingly, the line was halted."[110]

As the attack ended in the gathering darkness, the 60th New York Regiment found itself in advance of other assaulting regiments, within 70 yards of the Confederate works. The special problem here for the 60th was that the ridge they occupied had a lower elevation than that of the Confederates just ahead, therefore the New Yorkers must entrench on the *reverse crest* of the ridge rather than on the usual military crest on the forward slope. Colonel H. A. Barnum, commanding the 3rd Brigade that day described it this way: "The front line occupied a position about 150 yards from the rebel works (one regiment, the Sixtieth New York Volunteers, being less than 100 yards), protected partially by a rise of ground in front, but subjected to a cross-fire from an angle in the work in front of our right. About midnight the troops were withdrawn about 200 yards, and built breastworks."[111]

In the 15 June itinerary of the 60th New York, the regimental action is described as heavy resistance from the enemy's skirmishers for 2 or 3 miles, driving them into their main works near nightfall, and halting on a knoll nearby, the knoll giving them some protection while they "built works on this knoll with our bayonets and cups."[112] This shallow trench, fish-hooking at the western end, scratched out by the 60th New York that night in their frantic haste to protect themselves from the deadly cross-fire, can be seen today near the intersection of Hamilton and Kennesaw-Due West roads. When this trench was excavated several years ago, the large quantity of military gear recovered gave evidence of the fear and confusion of that moment in 1864. Recovered were hundreds of unfired bullets, a bayonet, a cartridge box tin (complete with US brass box plate and assorted brass brads with leather attached) containing a full issue of .58 caliber ammunition, several buckles with fragments of leather still attached, and New York manufactured gold-glazed military coat buttons, all attesting to that moment of crisis on a June evening. While Geary's division suffered nearly 600 casualties that day, neither Butterfield or Williams had pressed their attack and so experienced far fewer killed and wounded. Sherman's effort to find a point of weakness in the

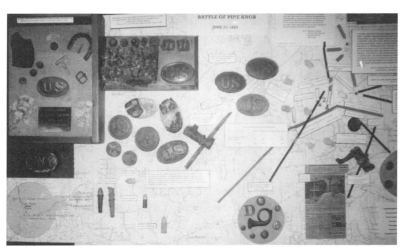

Many of these relics from the Battle of Pine Knob were recovered from the shallow trench of the 60th New York Regiment. Some of the items include three US cartridge box plates, a broken bayonet, and numerous bullets.

Confederate defenses near Lost Mountain had clearly failed. The character of the battle and the condition of Geary's division is succinctly described by Federal surgeon H. Earnest Goodman the day after the combat at Pine Knob:

> Condition of command: Worn out and exhausted by continual marching, building breast-works, and under continuous fire from May 25 [New Hope Church]. Roads heavy from rain for ten days. Battle begun 2 p.m.; continued six hours. Strength of command; Officers, 275; enlisted men, 4,752; total, 5,027; greater part engaged. Condition of supplies: Stimulants and surgical appliances rather scanty; difficult to obtain, because of very bad roads and worn out mules. Tents at hand all up, and wounded all sheltered. One continual rain after battle. Field hospital about two miles from line of attack; water abundant; food plenty. Operations: Amputation and resection, numbers unknown. Mode of removal of wounded: On stretchers and blankets to field surgeons; from there to ambulances; brought to hospitals during whole night. Character of the fire: Musketry and artillery; continuous; range 100 to 25 yards; enemy strongly entrenched; one continuous charge; enemy works…not carried; slaughter of Federals severe.[113]

While Hooker's XX army corps had little to show but a "bloody nose" for their failed attempt on the Confederate line near Lost Mountain on 15 June, McPherson had more success near Noonday Creek the same day. The 30th Illinois Regiment of Force's brigade (Leggett's division) had led the brigade dash across the creek, capturing a 320-strong Alabama regiment in its entirety. Overpowering this advance line at Noonday Creek, however, did not mean the Southerners were ready to abandon their principal line at Brushy Mountain. More than a week would elapse before such would transpire.

Now with the opponents once again locked in a tight military embrace, 16 June featured hard work for the infantry skirmish lines, artillery, and snipers. Captain Peter Simonson, commander of the 5th Indiana Battery and acting chief of artillery for the 1st Division of Howard's IV army corps, was busy that day placing a four-gun battery in a new forward position near the Confederate lines. A hundred yards away a rebel sniper equipped with a Whitworth rifle with telescopic sight could see Simonson in a prone position, rolling a small log ahead of him for protection from bullets as he sought a closer look at Confederate defenses. From the sniper's position Simonson's entire left side was exposed. The first shot missed; the second did not.[114] Simonson, whose 5th Indiana Battery two days before was reported to have fired the shot that killed General Polk, died instantly. The loss of the talents of this young officer was expressed in eulogies in the *Official Records* by several officers. Major General David S. Stanley, commander of the 1st Division wrote one of them: "This was an irreplaceable loss to the Division. I have not met an officer who was the equal of this one in energy, efficiency, and ingenuity in the handling of artillery. He never missed an opportunity and allowed no difficulties to deter him from putting in his batteries in every position that could prove annoying or destructive to the enemy."[115] In the predawn darkness of 17 June, the left flank of the Confederates was retired several miles nearer Kennesaw Mountain to a north-south position that covered the Burnt Hickory and Dallas roads. This new line hinged at a point near the Latimar House, forming a salient on a hill nearby, with Hardee's corps to the left of the position held by French's division of Polk's corps (now commanded by Loring). The set of fortifications from that point southward along the east bank of the creek, came to be called the "Mud Creek Line." It would be the primary line of battle from 17 through 19 June.

18

THE BATTLES
OF MUD CREEK AND
THE SAGA OF PETER CUPP

————◦•◦————

The salient on the hill at the point where Walker's division of Hardee's corps hinged with Samuel French's division of Polk's Army of Mississippi[116] created a right angle. Because of the right angle resulting from these intersecting lines, the defenses at French's hill were especially vulnerable to Federal artillery fire. In his diary, General French complained of the failure of Walker's skirmishers to defend the high ground near the Latimar House, resulting in his own skirmishers being forced to retire to the main line at the hill, to face a Federal "line of battle" that exposed his men to confront a crossfire of artillery and infantry "enfilading [the] line all day."[117]

The line of battle referred to by French was the result of an attack made by a reinforced skirmish line composed of the 26th Ohio, 57th Indiana, and the 100th Illinois regiments led by one-armed Colonel Frederick Bartleson. Bartleson was a veteran officer who had been wounded at Shiloh, captured at Chickamauga, and had just returned to service two weeks before, having been exchanged as prisoner of war from Richmond's infamous Libby Prison. On 18 June, the aggressive Bartleson, ignoring what was described as "one of the most terrific rain storms of the season," led his men in a charge through two waist-deep creeks to a low ridge in a large open field where they were momentarily stopped, experiencing heavy rifle fire from nearby Confederates. They then continued the charge to the next ridge where they overwhelmed the Confederate reserve skirmish line, taking several prisoners from Walker's division near the crest of the hill at the Latimar House. This position was less than 200 yards from the hill occupied by General French, the salient point in the Confederate "Mud Creek Line."

Since one of Bartleson's regiments was equipped with the seven-shot Spencer rifle, these troops had superior firepower. In the course of their charge, Bartleson had paused on a ridge in the open field, fired several volleys from their Spencers, then continued the charge to the second ridge near the Latimar House. During the charge across the field, several short rounds of artillery from Federal guns had fallen among them. This "friendly fire" experience apparently did little damage since many of these shells appeared to be a non-explosive round.[118] Two more regiments soon joined Bartleson's force, protecting his left flank and, by their presence, forcing French's pickets to give way as had Walker's a few minutes earlier. Twice during the night the Confederates made unsuccessful attempts to retake these trenches at the Latimar House. Bartleson's success that day had much to do with Johnston deciding to withdraw the next morning to the Confederate final line of defense at Kennesaw Mountain.[119]

There had also been Federal success at the south end of the Mud Creek entrenchments that day. Hardee had posted batteries of artillery on a bluff overlooking Mud Creek at the point where the Dallas-Marietta road crosses the stream; creating a military strong point at this southern end of the Mud Creek defenses. Hardee's guns at this fortress covered a mile or more of the open bottomland of the creek. Across from the bluff, on the west side of the creek, was a hill almost as high in elevation as the bluff. Here, protected by the crest of the hill, Captain Giles J. Cockerill, Battery "D" of the 1st Ohio Artillery, began firing with "nothing but the muzzles of the guns…visible from the front." Cockerill maintained an hour-long artillery duel with Hardee's guns at the near-point-blank range of less than 200 yards. Hardee's guns were soon silenced and the fort left in shambles. Colonel Lucius Polk, nephew of General Polk, the com-

The Latimar House on Kirk Lane has been enlarged and improved over the years, but close examination of the structure suggests that a substantial portion of the original house remains. In the woods nearby is the line of shallow trenches captured by Col. Bartleson and his Spencer-wielding soldiers on 18 June.

mander of the fort, was seriously wounded and permanently disabled in this action.[120]

And so it was in the pre-dawn hours of 19 June, that the Mud Creek line was abandoned by the Confederates. The new line of defense became Kennesaw Mountain, with the flanks on Brushy Mountain eastward, and trailing southward across the Powder Springs Road near the Kolb House.

Private Peter Cupp of Company H, 15th Ohio, was a member of a squad of Federal soldiers assigned to round up stragglers in the now-abandoned Confederate trenches. Cupp was having quite a day. With two or three of these Confederate stragglers in hand, Cupp was ordered by his sergeant to escort the prisoners to the rear. Rounding a corner in the trench Cupp nearly collided with a company of Confederate infantry. In the darkness assuming at first that these were fellow Federals, he discovered that they were instead Confederates. A conversation then ensued in which:

> Cupp with great coolness and address explained to the captain commanding the company the condition of things; that his [the captain's] friends had left and that four companies of ours had entered their works and were between him and his friends [which to say the least was something of an exaggeration], and that the best thing he could do was surrender. Cupp's prisoners and his close proximity to the works corroborating his story, the captain concluding that "discretion was the better part of valor," surrendered himself, Captain S. Yates Levy, his lieutenant, and 17 men, Company D, 1st Georgia Regiment of Volunteers, prisoners of war, and Cupp placing himself at their head marched them into our lines.[121]

With this and with several other similar episodes, the trenches along Mud Creek were cleared of Confederates and secured by the Federals. By 19 June, with the Mud Creek defensive line now abandoned, the next eleven days of June would be characterized by cavalry battles on the Bells Ferry and Canton roads, brigade- and division-size fighting along the Burnt Hickory Road, and the battles at Kolb Farm and Kennesaw Mountain.

19

THE WALLIS HOUSE AND BATTLE OF NODINE'S HILL

In 1850, Josiah Wallis came to Cobb County and purchased land lot 290 containing 160 acres along Burnt Hickory Road. By 1853, he had constructed a comfortable frame house consisting of five rooms with a central hall and two chimneys. A log kitchen with a cooking fire place and chimney was constructed nearby. The Wallis family refugeed in June, 1864.

On 19 June, Major General Oliver O. Howard, commander of the Federal IV Army Corps, notified Sherman that his headquarters was now at "Wallace's [Wallis] house on the Marietta [Burnt Hickory] road." In the days immediately preceding 19 June, the Wallis house had been used as a Confederate field hospital for the nearby battles of Latimore's Farm and Mud Creek. Soldiers who died while at the Wallis house were buried across the road in a peach orchard on what is today the property of Mrs. Ruby Walker.[122] When the Confederate line moved eastward to nearby Kennesaw Mountain on the 19 June, the Wallis House and the hill behind it continued to be used as a command center, signal station, and a telegraph relay exchange. Since the house was located at the halfway point between Brushy Mountain in the east and the southernmost Federal activities near the Kolb House on the Powder Springs Road, Sherman spent a lot of time here with General Howard. And the battles on the nearby ridges were directed from this command center at the Wallis

House. The boundaries of these battles are roughly Burnt Hickory Road on the north, today's Mt. Calvary Road on the west, Dallas Road on the south, and the present-day Kennesaw Mountain National Battlefield Park boundary on the east. This field of combat is essentially rectangular. Chief among the terrain features is Noyes' Creek. This is ordinarily a small stream which rises in the area out of spring-fed marshy ground and flows in several small channels generally west to southwest, in effect dividing the battlefield rectangle at its midsection. In 1864, because of two weeks of heavy rains, 19 June found this stream a torrent.[123] On a large ridge-like hill we now call "Whitaker's" are "horseshoe-shaped" battle entrenchments. These are located north and east of the several branches of Noyes' Creek in that vicinity. "Bald Knob"(aka Nodine's or Artillery Hill) is about 100 yards due south of Whitaker's Hill, the stream dividing the two. On 20 June, Howard ordered military assaults simultaneously on these two hills.

Walter Whitaker, commanding the 2nd Brigade of the 1st Division of the IV Army Corps, described the ground from which he launched this attack as a swamp in which his skirmishers were having to wade in water above their knees—a position in which the enemy's artillery could enfilade the Federal lines as far as the range of their guns.[124] At 4:00 P.M. the assault began. The attack was conducted so aggressively that the "bulk of the rebels occupying the works were killed or taken prisoners." No sooner had the Federals gained these works, however, than the Confederates sent in two fresh regiments to regain the fortification. Failing this, additional reinforcements were brought in by both contest-

Battles near the Wallis House on the hills overlooking nearby Noses Creek were targets of heavy artillery barrages. General Sherman's report shows the expenditure of thousands of artillery shells during the Atlanta Campaign in 1864. This storage bin contains a portion of the shell fragments recovered from the battle trail from Ringgold to Jonesboro. Many of these fragments are from the Wallis House vicinity.

The Wallis House was the battlefield headquarters of General Oliver Otis Howard (IV Army Corp commander) from 19 June until after the Battle of Kennesaw Mountain on 27 June. The Wallis House is expected to become a satellite of Kennesaw Mountain National Battlefield Park.

ants, the battle continuing until near midnight. Friend and foe being mixed, it was "a most fiercely and deadly contested battle ground." Five Federal companies on the right of the 35th Indiana were overwhelmed by superior numbers and driven from the captured works, "the enemy gain[ing] a lodgment in my line":

> In two instances coming under my observation the bayonets of the loyal and rebel soldiers were found in each other's person. My loss was 273 killed, wounded, and missing. The enemy's loss was reported to me as between 500 and 600 killed and over 1000 wounded. Among the missing is Lieutenant-Colonel Watson, of the Fortieth Ohio, who in the darkness charged the rebel lines and with several of his men were surrounded and captured. The fight took place on one of the spurs of Kennesaw Mountain.[125]

In conjunction with Whitaker's fight on the ridge north of Noyes' Creek, Colonel Issac Kirby, 101st Ohio Infantry, in command of the 1st Brigade, advanced to seize Bald Knob on the south side of the creek. Kirby carried the hill despite heavy rifle and artillery fire but not having time to entrench, and with flanks not properly secured, the Confederates managed to retake the hill. The hill changed hands three times and by darkness, the rebels remained in control of the crest. General Stanley decided against further attempts to storm the hill that evening. The next morning from his command post at the Wallis House, Howard instructed Stanley to order Kirby's Brigade, reinforced by Colonel Nodine's, to try again. Howard's official report described the two-brigade battle this way:

> At 11:30 a.m. I ordered that Colonel Kirby and Colonel Nodine, commanding General Wood's left brigade, move in conjunction, and seize and hold the Bald Knob that Kirby had lost the evening before. The enemy had then entrenched it pretty strongly, and it was under the hottest kind of fire from his guns. I directed a concentrated artillery fire of a half hour's duration upon this point, and ordered the advance, which was promptly made. The enemy was driven off, a number of prisoners were taken, the knob secured, and the crest entrenched while the enemy was firing upon it from two batteries of artillery.[126]

With the Federals in firm control, the battle of Nodine's Hill (a.k.a. Bald Knob or Artillery Hill) was history.

The Wallis family returned to their home at the end of the war to find the house standing but badly damaged by the hard use of its wartime occupants—Confederate hospital and Federal military headquarters. The house was soon repaired and Josiah Wallis and his wife continued to make their home there until his death in 1875, and her death ten years later. The couple is buried at the nearby New Salem Church cemetery. In 1947, a great granddaughter purchased the house and refurbished the structure. The granddaughter, Julia Hairston, and her husband, Roy Lovingood, reared their three children in this house. Julia died in 1982 and her husband in 2000.

This collection of battle artifacts from Nodine's Hill in Cobb County was gathered during the 1960s and include a Confederate Reed artillery shell and one cannonball. Two Federal Schenkle shells complete with marked brass fuse, and a chain strap from a cannon carriage are in this picture. Perhaps one of the best battlefield recoveries of the author's nearly forty-five years of searching is the nice brass lance point from a battle flag at Nodine's Hill.

By 23 June 1864, the Wallis House and the nearby fields of battle passed into history. The house today (2006) has survived both war and time. Recently, preservationist in Cobb County won a victory with a cooperating real estate developer. The Wallis House initially had been set aside from the nearby residential development as a history preserve. Recently, the family has decided to place the house on the real estate market instead. Recently, the Cobb County Board of Commissioners, the superintendent of the Kennesaw Mountain National Battlefield Park, and the Georgia Civil War Commission have succeeded in putting together some "green space" and state "trails" monies to purchase the historic Wallis House (2 +/-acres), with Cobb County as temporary owner. The Federal government will eventually own and govern the site as a satellite of the Kennesaw Mountain National Battlefield Park in the future.

SANDTOWN ROAD
AND THE MANNING HOUSE

The Mannings had settled along the Sandtown Road in west Cobb County. In 1852, the Manning family had migrated from the Chester District (Columbia), South Carolina, acquiring over 1000 acres in west Cobb County, and building a water-powered grist mill on the nearby Noyes Creek at the Sandtown Road crossing of the stream. Planning to continue planting cotton as he had in South Carolina, Simpson Manning had brought seventeen slaves, including several house servants, with him. The grist mill at the creek was to be a convenience for his neighbors and an additional source of income for the family.

Manning's oldest son Jacob had preceded the family to Cobb County by a couple of years, locating and buying property for himself and the Manning family along the Sandtown Road. He built a double-crib, two-story hand-hewn log house for himself, the structure remaining into the twentieth century until taken down by a developer in the 1980s.

Construction began on the Simpson Manning family house in 1852. The building is a four-room basic structure built around a central hallway, with a stairway leading to a second floor large single room. This room, by custom, was considered the "dormitory bedroom" for the pre-pubescent children. A separate building housed the cooking fireplace and kitchen. Nearby a well was dug. The house was considered a "brace-frame" style construction, meaning large hand-hewn support timbers of pine and poplar, with mortise and tendon bracing with pegs. The house included five fireplaces constructed of handmade brick formed and fired at the site. This house, simple in design and construction, was typical of the "starter house" for the westward-moving planter. The idea was that if things went well, the house would be enlarged with wings added as needed. If the economics of the location did not work, then the family would continue to migrate westward into new lands in Alabama and Mississippi. The romantic image of the grand house with white columns in north Georgia with magnolias nearby is simply more myth than reality. The Simpson Manning House remains today as proof of the less ostentatious and more practical nature of a great many of the slaveholding middle class farmers in the antebellum South.

Time and events would work against the Mannings on the Sandtown Road. By 1861, the three Manning sons would be in Confederate military service. One of the three, Charles, would die of a fever in a military camp in Virginia, and by 1863 one of the Manning teenage daughters would succumb to a similar condition. Simpson Manning would pass away the

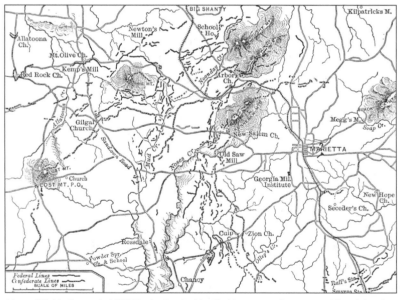

Map of Cobb County in 1864. The landmarks identified here are quite accurate (Cox, Atlanta).

same year, leaving the widow with seemingly no recourse but to return with her remaining two daughters to their previous home near Columbia, South Carolina. The surviving Manning sons would return from Virginia in 1865 to war-torn homes and trench-worn farmlands. The family would remain in the Cobb County community as popular leaders into the twenty-first century.

So it was that when Sherman's Army of the Ohio moved down the Sandtown Road in 1864, the Mannings no longer occupied their house. A servant remained to tell Federal military officials of the owners. The *Official Records* tell us that a Federal brigade entrenched near the Manning house, and from an inspection of the building today, we see physical evidence of battle in a bullet lodged in the front door jam and blood stains on the floors—a graphic record telling us of the use made of

The Simpson Manning House appears here at its original location on the West Sandtown Road. The house was moved to the Due West community in west Cobb County in 1975 and restored. The Cobb County Fire Department was preparing to burn the house for practice (unaware of its historic value) in 1975, and a residential development was planned for the site on West Sandtown Road. The house was lifted one story to provide more living space, but otherwise rules of historic restoration were observed.

the house during the battles around Manning's Mill on 20–21 June 1864.[127] Cox's division of the Army of the Ohio was the unit primarily involved at the battle of Manning's Mill. Opposed by Ross's Confederate cavalry near the mill, but more seriously opposed by the raging torrent of the rain-swollen Noyes' Creek, Cox was unable to force a crossing until 21 June. Cox's division then moved east to the Cheney House while Hascal's division proceeded further eastward along the Macland Road directly into the battle of Kolb's Farm.

The Manning House was built in 1852 by Simpson Manning, a patriarch of a slave-owning, middle-class farming family. The house was damaged during the nearby battle of Manning's Mill on 19 June 1864, but survived the years, and in 1976 was moved to west Cobb County where it was restored and today is the private home of Phil and Kay Secrist.

21

COLONEL BARNHILL AT KENNESAW SPUR, 27 JUNE

The Kolb Farm battle on 22 June was the result of an overzealous effort by General Hood to stem the tide of Federal units flanking south across the Powder Springs Road west of Marietta. Early that day, Hooker's XX corps was sideling southward from the Dallas Road, across Ward Creek Valley, striking Powder Springs Road near the Kolb house. Westward from Sandtown Road, Hascall's division was approaching the nearby intersection of Macland and Powder Springs roads at the Atkinson plantation, a classic Greek-columned-style building located on a hill about 200 yards west of Kolb's farmhouse.

Hood's corps had been transferred from Brushy Mountain two nights before to assist in extending the Confederate left southward to keep pace with Sherman's flanking movements in that direction. The battle of Kolb's farm was an independent blocking action initiated by Hood, unsanctioned by Confederate commander Johnston, an action that can only be described as a dismal failure in every sense which cost Hood more than 1000 casualties. The defeat was a two-hour product of deadly crossfire by Federal artillery posted on the hills overlooking the killing ground in the Ward Creek Valley. The battle at Kolb farm achieved two things. Hood's description of the battle as a victory rather than the defeat it was further reduced his standing with General Johnston, and secondly, the battle at Kolb farm, temporarily frustrating Sherman's flanking strategy, may have contributed to Sherman's decision to attack the principal Kennesaw Mountain defenses on 27 June. On 24 June, Sherman published the Kennesaw attack orders. The XV Army Corps (McPherson's), which had been transferred from the Brushy Mountain sector, was now astride the Burnt Hickory Road near the Kirk House, and within 300 yards of its target. Kennesaw Hill (now called Pigeon Hill), a spur of Little Kennesaw was this target. A 5000-man attack force was to sweep over this hill near the junction of Walker's (Hardee's corps) and French's divisions. Should they be successful, Marietta and the railroad lay as prizes just beyond. The entire Confederate line must surely be abandoned.

A thirty-minute artillery barrage preceded the 8:00 A.M. infantry attack. Directly in the path of this attack were the pickets of the 63rd Georgia. The battle line of the assaulting lead unit, 53rd Ohio, was upon the Georgians before they knew it. Colonel Robert Fulton commanding the 53rd described later how his regiment found themselves in a hand-to-hand fight where "bayonets and butts of muskets were used."[128] Another source tells of a meeting in this melee between an Irish rebel and a "stout" Federal soldier who had seized the rebel's gun by the barrel; "The two had quite a struggle for the prize, when Pat [a general ethnic reference], perceiving that the Federal soldier was about to get the best of him, with the exclamation, 'To hell with you and the gun!' gave his opponent a sudden shove which threw him to the ground, and then taking to his heels made his escape."[129] A lieutenant in the 63rd escaped capture by shooting one of his opponents, disabling another with his sword, and thrusting a third out of the way. "His clothing was riddled but he came off unscathed." Some eighty or so of the 63rd Georgia were killed, wounded, or captured in this action on the 27th. The next day, a reserve force of pickets from the 63rd charged and retook the rifle-pits lost the day before, then fought from them for several hours before being forced to abandon them later in the day. In this second day's action, two Confederates were killed and nine wounded, and nine more were cut off in an angle of the works and captured. The conduct of the 63rd Georgia was noted and complimented in official correspondence by General W. H. T. Walker on the 27th and 28th.[130]

Lieutenant Colonel Rigdon S. Barnhill was leading the 40th Illinois in this attack on 27 June at Kennesaw Hill. Barnhill's unit hit the gorge between the hill and Little Kennesaw Mountain. As he approached the gorge, his unit came under intense fire from the front and both flanks, causing him to veer to the right, directly up the rocky slope of Kennesaw Hill. Straight ahead, Cockrell's Confederates of French's division "poured a deadly fire into the ranks of the advancing 40th Illinois." Less than 30 feet from the Confederates, Barnhill was struck by a bullet to the head, dying instantly—too close to the rebel trench for his body to be recovered by the Federals.[131]

Meanwhile, 2 miles south of Kennesaw Hill, near the Dallas Road, Cleburne's and Cheatham's divisions were being attacked by 12,000 Federal soldiers from Thomas's Army of the Cumberland. Here was the heaviest fighting of the day. Confederate Sam Watkins remembered how a hundred Federal guns targeted his regiment's position for more than an hour, followed by the rush of a solid line of bluecoats:

> My pen is unable to describe the scene of carnage and death that ensued in the next two hours. Column after column of Federal soldiers were crowded upon that line…but no sooner would a regiment mount our works then they were shot down or surrendered….Yet still the Yankees came. The sun beaming down on our uncovered heads, the thermometer being one hundred degrees in the shade, and a solid line of blazing fire right from the muzzles of the Yankee guns being poured into our very faces. Afterward I heard a soldier express himself by saying that he thought "Hell had broke loose in Georgia, sure enough."[132]

Sam Watkin's Tennessee regiment held its ground that day. Down the line to the right, Cleburne's division was holding its ground also. During the height of the battle, the woods in front of these fortifications caught fire endangering the helpless Federal wounded nearby. A fifteen-minute ceasefire was extended by the Confederates to allow the wounded to be

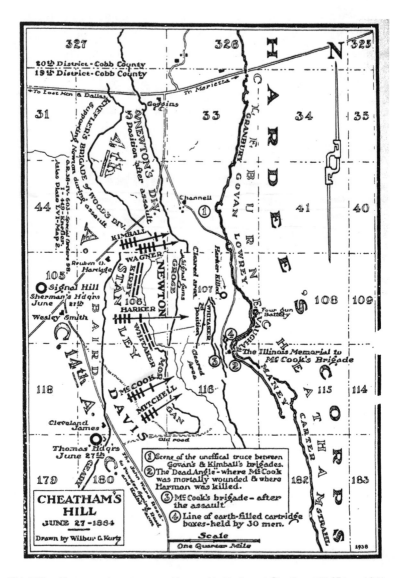

This Wilbur Kurtz map shows troop positions and battle lines at Cheatham Hill, 27 June 1864.

The visitor's center at Kennesaw Mountain National Battlefield Park.

rescued; Yanks and Rebs alike assisting in this humanitarian effort. A "thank you" by the nearest Federal officer, then the carnage of battle was resumed.[133]

Earlier on the morning of 27 June, the 86th Illinois principal musician, Fife Major Alason Webber, had borrowed a Henry rifle and 120 rounds of ammunition from his regimental commander. Webber's use of this weapon that day earned him the Medal of Honor. The citation reads, "Voluntarily joined in a charge against the enemy, which was repulsed, and by his rapid firing in the face of the enemy enabled many of the wounded to return to the

The Illinois Monument at Cheatham Hill is one of the most interesting spots in Kennesaw Mountain National Battlefield Park and was erected by the aging veterans of the battle in the early twentieth century. It marks the spot of heavy combat described by Sam Watkins.

The Cheney House on Sandtown Road was a military landmark in 1864 and served as General John Schofield's headquarters through much of the fighting around Kennesaw Mountain. General Sherman planned much of the Battle of Kennesaw Mountain here. The Cheney house was built c.1856, but was damaged by hard use during the military activities. The house required substantial repair and restoration by the 1920s. The house and 9 acres of grounds were for sale in 2003.

Federal lines, with others, held the advance of the enemy while temporary works were being constructed."[134]

By 11:00 A.M. the battle of Kennesaw Mountain was over. Except for Cox and Hascall gaining a key crossroad beyond Olley Creek on the extreme southern flank, 27 June had few rewards for Sherman—and 3000 casualties. The Confederate loss in killed, wounded, and captured was about 500; once again the "spade and the fort" had won over raw human courage. Within forty-eight hours, Sherman had resumed his flanking tactics, shifting his army westward in such a way as to capitalize on the crossroads gained past Olley Creek on 27 June, in the direction of Smyrna and the Chattahoochee River. With their railroad and line of retreat thus threatened, the Confederates abandoned the Kennesaw Mountain fortifi-

The McAdoo House, called the Atkinson Plantation after the War, was built c.1855. Called "Melora" during the war years, it is located on the battlefield of Kolb Farm and was a Federal headquarters during the battle. The McAdoo family lived here briefly in 1863, and it was here that William G. McAdoo was born, a future member of President Wilson's cabinet and a "would be presidential candidate" in the 1920s The house had been restored and was for sale as of 2003.

cations on 3 July, giving up Marietta, and retreating slowly along the railroad toward Atlanta. The battleground in the Atlanta Campaign had been Cobb County since 3 June. Now, between 4 and 16 July, the scene of action would shift south to the Chattahoochee and beyond. But first, a unique complex of defensive bunkers called "shoupades," forming a Confederate bridgehead on the north bank of the river, from Vinings westward to Mayson-Turners Ferry Road (Veteran's Parkway), would be the challenge.

ROSWELL WOMEN AND THE JOHNSTON RIVER LINE

The Johnston River line consisted of "shoupades" and a 6-mile arc of other fortifications at the river, described as a series of block houses built of logs, double walled, with the space between packed with dirt. These block houses contained artillery sighted with interlocking fields of fire, and were connected by palisaded logs rising in several tiers providing clear fields of fire for use by infantry. This unique and powerful line of works was anchored on the river on the east at the railroad crossing at Vinings, and on the west at the river near Nickajack Creek.[135]

Before these entrenchments would be reached on 5 July, the Federal army had occupied Marietta, the battle of Smyrna had been fought on 4 July, and the Army of the Ohio had begun its march to the river fords near Roswell. General Thomas (commander of the Army of the Cumberland) established his headquarters at the Georgia Military Institute just south of the Marietta city square on Sunday, 3 July. Regiment after regiment of Federal soldiers marched through town that day and the day following, along the railroad and main wagon road leading south toward Smyrna and the Chattahoochee River. Thomas issued orders on 5 June "[t]o preserve public and private property in Marietta as nearly as possible in the state in which [it was found], and to prevent plundering and pillaging. You will arrest all deserters and strag-

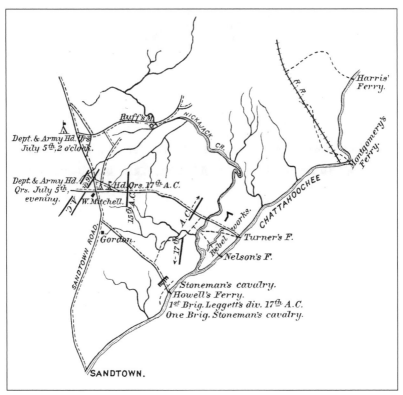

This map shows the position of the XVII Army Corps near the Mitchell House and the Johnston River Line *(Official Atlas of the Civil War)*.

glers and forward those belonging to the Army of the Cumberland to these headquarters by squads of from thirty to fifty…. You will permit no officer to take quarters in Marietta, except by order of Major General Sherman."[136]

Marietta was now a garrison town under military rule by an invading army. The town would escape fire and destruction until fall that year. Then in November, the courthouse on the square and all buildings facing the square would be burned by the departing Federals leaving intact only the Masonic building at the southwest corner, and the damaged Kennesaw House a block off the square near the railroad.[137]

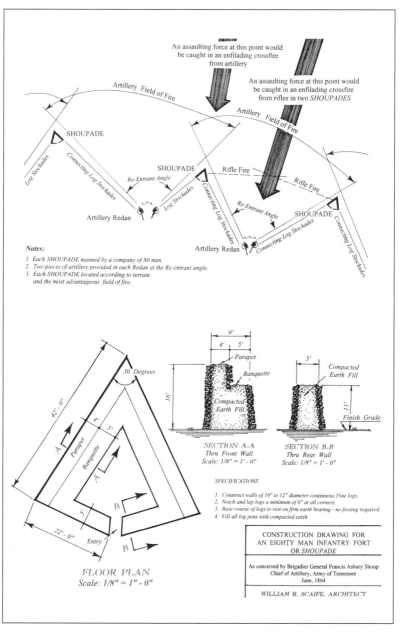

An assaulting force at this point would be caught in an enfilading crossfire from artillery

An assaulting force at this point would be caught in an enfilading crossfire from rifles in two *SHOUPADES*

Artillery *Field of Fire*

Artillery *Field of Fire*

SHOUPADE

Log Stockades

Connecting Log Stockades

SHOUPADE

Re-Entrant Angle

Log Stockades

Rifle Fire

Rifle Fire

Connecting Log Stockades

Re-Entrant Angle

Artillery Redan

SHOUPADE

Connecting Log Stockades

Artillery Redan

Connecting Log Stockades

Notes:
1. Each SHOUPADE manned by a company of 80 men.
2. Two pieces of artillery provided in each Redan at the Re-entrant angle.
3. Each SHOUPADE located according to terrain and the most advantageous field of fire.

30 Degrees

42'- 0"

Parapet

Banquette

4"

5'

16'

5'

22'- 0"

Entry

FLOOR PLAN
Scale: 1/8" = 1" - 0"

9'

4'   5'

Parapet

Banquette

Compacted Earth Fill

SECTION A-A
Thru Front Wall
Scale: 1/8" = 1' - 0"

5'

Compacted Earth Fill

11'

Finish Grade

SECTION B-B
Thru Rear Wall
Scale: 1/8" = 1' - 0"

SPECIFICATIONS

1. Construct walls of 10" to 12" diameter continuous Pine logs.
2. Notch and lap logs a minimum of 6" at all corners.
3. Base course of logs to rest on firm earth bearing - no footing required.
4. Fill all log pens with compacted earth.

CONSTRUCTION DRAWING FOR
AN EIGHTY MAN INFANTRY FORT
OR *SHOUPADE*

As conceived by Brigadier General Francis Asbury Shoup
Chief of Artillery, Army of Tennessee
June, 1864

WILLIAM R. SCAIFE, ARCHITECT

(top) Military concept of the river line. (bottom) Architectural drawing of a shoupade.

The movement of armies toward the Chattahoochee River placed the Army of the Cumberland directly along the railroad, and the armies of the Tennessee and the Ohio along the Sandtown Road. Marching columns of soldiers characterized activities in Cobb County between 3 and 8 July. The Confederates delayed the movement to the river with an entrenched line at Smyrna, extending from Rottenwood Creek on the east, running west, crossing the railroad, and then following the ridge to near the point of the Old Concord/Concord roads intersection, where it then hooked south for a short distance. This line of fortifications at Smyrna terminated in the west at the "fish hook" about 2 miles east of the bridge on Nickajack Creek at Ruff's Mill.[138] At 4:00 P.M. on 4 July, a column of six regiments from Dodge's XVI army corps, led by Colonel E. F. Noyes of the 39th Ohio Infantry, charged the Confederates, striking the angle of the fortifications near the crossroads, capturing an advanced line of trenches and about 100 prisoners. The Federals experienced 140 casualties themselves, including Colonel Noyes whose leg was amputated. The next day, with the Confederates abandoning these defenses during the night, the XVI Army Corps followed the retreating Southern army, camping for the evening at the Widow Mitchell's house on the Sandtown Road.[139]As the principal activities of the armies in west Cobb County moved toward the Chattahoochee River, Sherman was simultaneously transferring the Army of the Ohio eastward in search of river crossings near Roswell. Cox's division was able to make such a crossing at Soap Creek on a fish dam, capturing a cannon, and surprising and routing the Confederate pickets—thus, the first bridgehead on the south side of the river. Dodge's XVI corps was not far behind. They marched to Roswell a day later than Cox, and then started building a 650-feet long trestle bridge for Federal infantry. Forty-eight hours later the bridge was ready for use.

Just prior to these river crossings, Sherman's cavalry under Garrard had swept through Roswell, burning the cotton and woolen mills, and corralling the 400 female mill workers. These workers were then transported to Marietta. Sherman was surprised to learn these factories were still operating, supposing that the machinery had been dismantled and shipped south. He ordered Garrard to arrest all:

People, male and female, no matter what the clamor, and let them foot it, under guard, to Marietta [15 miles], whence I will send them by cars [rail] to the North. Destroy and make the same disposition of all mills save flouring mills manifestly for local use, but all saw mills and factories dispose of effectually, and useful laborers, excused by reason of their skill as manufacturers from conscription, are as much prisoners as if armed. The poor women will make a howl. Let them take along their children and clothing, providing they have the means of hauling or you can spare them. We will retain them until they can reach a country where they can live in peace and security.[140]

In Marietta these pawns of war were joined by 200 more with their children from the New Manchester Mills in the southwest corner of Cobb County. Sherman then ordered these 600 women and children transported north to Louisville and beyond; as he said, across the Ohio River where they could be "turned loose to earn a living where they won't do us any harm."[141] Thus we find an example of Sherman's philosophy of modern war in the official records: a conviction that an army in the field is sustained by a civilian workforce at home, making them equally the adversary.

With two bridgeheads south of the river by 12 July and the Confederates abandoning the north bank of the Chattahoochee and retiring toward the outer defenses of Atlanta, Sherman's "chess game" of war was in high gear. On that day, he wrote McPherson telling how he thought it possible to maneuver in such a way as to cause Johnston to weaken either his center or his flanks. Should he weaken his right Sherman would go for the Augusta Railroad, if Johnston should weaken his center, Atlanta would be open for the taking, and if Johnston should go on the offensive then "we cover our roads and base and...make as good use of Peach Tree Creek as he."[142] The Atlanta newspapers of 10 July reported that there had been a "council of war that day" and "that Johnston would make a fight for the city." But everything else showed differently: "All trains belonging to the army have gone to Augusta, and everybody fleeing." [143] Sherman's orders for crossing the river came down on 13 July. The final drama in the experience of wartime Atlanta was about to begin.

ATLANTA: THE BATTLES AT PEACHTREE CREEK

In Atlanta, not everybody was fleeing, only those who could. From a refugee-swelled population of 20,000 in January 1864, by early July the exodus from the fair city had reduced the civilian population to less than 3,000. As the population scattered before the converging columns of Sherman's blue-coated soldiers, the stress of war widened the cracks of public and private morale.

The fissures had appeared early in the war as profiteering flourished. By 1864, the unsatisfactory methods of Confederate financing, the inadequate production and distribution of consumer goods, and the military reverses all contributed to soaring prices and plunging morale. Most people justified their resistance to policies such as conscription and impressments because of what they considered inherent injustices in the laws. The war weariness that gripped Georgia by 1864 was well illustrated by the response to Governor Brown's appeal for all men to come forward for military service in the summer when Sherman was pressing at the very doors of Atlanta. Confederate Congressman Benjamin H. Hill agreed with President Davis that Brown's appeal went unheeded to the extent that not more than one-third of the men eligible in the state were in the field.[144]

Since the city was under martial law, citizens of Atlanta were particularly harassed by military regulations. Passes were required to move about the city after dark, or to leave or enter the city at any hour.[145]

It was inevitable that military officials responsible for enforcing the regulations would arouse displeasure. On one such occasion in 1864, however, the military-pass inspector was frustrated in his duty. Captain William A. Fuller, the conductor-hero of the Andrew's Raid two years before, was offended by the manner in which the pass-inspector was carrying out his responsibilities. The inspector had used abusive language during a dispute with a group of ladies in Fuller's coach. The incident had arisen over what the ladies considered an unjust confiscation of their passes. When Fuller reprimanded the inspector for his conduct, the angry official ordered the guard to arrest the gallant conductor. This proved more difficult to accomplish than might be supposed, since most of the guard were intoxicated at the moment. Captain Fuller was able to make good his escape and reach the office of the provost marshall who, upon hearing Fuller's account, ordered the immediate arrest of the unpleasant inspector and his entire guard, much to the delight of the city's oft-abused citizens.[146]

Military deferments constituted another major source of dissention. S. P. Richards reported in his diary on 20 January 1864, with obvious satisfaction, that he had managed to obtain a printer's exemption despite the weakness of his claim.[147] Richards successfully escaped active military duty at the front, but he was soon required to enroll in the local printer's militia and thus compelled to perform guard duty during the weeks of summer crisis.[148] By August 1864, Richards and other male citizens who had elected to remain in the city during the siege found little time to pursue their normal business activities. Fighting fires produced by the incoming artillery shells employed the labor of every able-bodied man in one or another of the four volunteer fire units. Firefighting was especially hazardous in August since Union gunners seemed to take special pleasure in shelling burning buildings. It is surprising to learn that no fireman lost his life in the line of duty during the siege.[149] With the river crossed, and Atlanta just ahead, Sherman had several new concerns. The Confederate commander had been replaced on 17 July by John Bell Hood, and Hood was less cautious than Johnston. Also, just ahead was Peachtree Creek, a considerable stream to be crossed before Atlanta proper could be reached.

On 19 June, the Army of the Cumberland had crossed the creek less than 5 miles from Atlanta. To his left was Schofield's Army of the Ohio, and on Schofield's left was McPherson's Army of the Tennessee. The Ohio and Tennessee armies were part of a wheeling movement that would bring them into Atlanta from the east via Decatur and the Augusta Railroad with the Cumberland army the pivot. Hardee's and Stewart's Confederates led the attack astride Tanyard Branch aiming for the Peachtree Creek troop crossing now in progress, hoping to catch the Federals at a disadvantage while in the act of bridging the stream. Because of the difficult terrain and the absence of good maps, the attack was delayed two hours while troop positions were extended eastward to cover a reported threat to that flank. The attack focused on Newton's division, and the seam between Ward's and Geary's divisions, and continued with repeated assaults until nightfall. On one occasion Maney's and Loring's divisions striking this seam "were met with canister from Geary's batteries and with infantry fire in front and flank. They lost their organization, and were fearfully slaughtered. Few battlefields of the war have been strewn so thickly with dead and wounded as they lay the evening around Collier's Mill."[150]

The battle at Peachtree Creek cost the Confederates more than 5,000 casualties; the Federal forces around 2,000. Here was Hood's opening shot as commander; the first of what would be three colossal failures in the course of ten days. Before the month was out, the Confederate army's strength would be reduced by nearly 20,000.

The Peachtree battle site at Collier's Mill is now a posh neighborhood of fine homes in the Buckhead area of Atlanta. A small pocket park near Tanyard Branch, with markers and tablets commemorating the battle action on 20 July 1864, is all that remains of the site. Nearby historical markers on several streets help visitors follow the flow of battle.

Near the end of the Peachtree Creek battle, Hood had ordered Cleburne's division east toward Decatur to slow McPherson's progress from Decatur. Wheeler's cavalry was being overwhelmed by Union infantry at a hill just east of Atlanta. Doggedly, Wheeler's men held on until Cleburne's veteran division arrived. The position was held that evening, but heavy fighting continued next day for this "bald hill." Cleburne's division, forced to surrender the hill, would return the next day to have another go at it in the Battle of Atlanta, 22 July 1864—the bloodiest battle in the Atlanta Campaign. After 22 July, the bald hill would be renamed "Leggett's Hill," forever memorialized in blood that day and today as the center scene in the great painting, the Cyclorama.

These Collier's Mill items help mark the vicinity of the small history preserve at the site of the Battle of Peachtree Creek. The neighborhood is now an upscale community in north Atlanta.

24

THE BATTLE OF ATLANTA, 22 JULY 1864

Hood's plan for the battle on 22 July was to strike McPherson's flank and rear at Bald Hill by bringing Hardee's corps out of Atlanta via a 15-mile night-long march over back roads. This attack was intended to surprise the Federal, striking their entrenchments shortly before daylight on 22 July. Such a bold maneuver was reminiscent of Jackson and Lee at Chancellorsville the year before. Because of bad roads, nighttime misdirection on marching routes, and the exhaustion of Hardee's battle-weary troops, the four Confederate divisions were not in place to attack until nearly 1:00 P.M.

Cleburne and Maney's divisions struck the flank and front of the Federal divisions of Smith and Leggett (XVII Army Corps) near the intersection of today's Flat Shoals and Glenwood avenues. It was here that Major General James McPherson was killed early in the battle as he rode toward the sound of battle and into a line of Confederate skirmishers who shot him as he tried to escape. Walker and Bates's divisions, on Cleburne's right, struggled out of the thickets and marshes at Terry Mill Pond a few minutes earlier only to collide unexpectedly with Sweeney's division of the Federal XVI Army Corps. This division, on its way to reinforce the XVII Corps on Bald Hill, had stopped to rest moments before on an eminence overlooking the Sugar Creek Valley in precisely the right position to blunt the attack by Walker and Bates, an attack that was

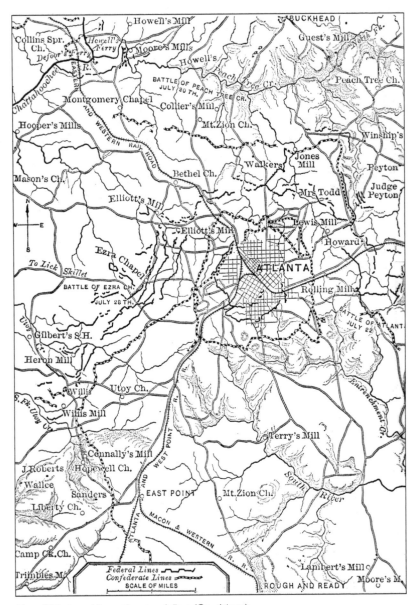

Map of Atlanta and its wartime trench lines (Cox, *Atlanta*).

intended to strike the rear of the XVII Corps. It was here that Major General W. H. T. Walker was killed.

Angry and frustrated by the ineptness of a local guide whom he thought responsible for the delays in his march, Walker, having just emerged from the thickets at Sugar Creek, was in the act of forming his division to deal with Sweeney, when he was killed instantly by a nearby Federal sharpshooter: "Walker rode out from the woods, and swinging his hat, cheered his men forward, but the next moment he was shot from his horse. Here the slaughter was fearful, as many as thirteen of Walker's men being found dead in one corner of a rail fence behind which they formed."[151] Fuller's division of Dodge's XVII corps happened also to be nearby and caught much of the brunt of the attack by Walker's division, but "lay down behind a ridge, and aided by artillery from their rear, managed to hold their ground until withdrawn at night. Sweeny's division that day lost 208, and Fuller's 653, killed, wounded and missing."[152]

Walker's division also lost heavily that day. Mercer's brigade alone suffered 168 casualties, the 63rd Georgia among the units hardest hit. The casualties in Walker's division were so great on 22 July that the division was broken up, the remnants assigned to other units, principally to Cleburne and Cheatham.

Throughout the afternoon on 22 July, the Confederate attacks continued. Several Federal units were driven from their entrenchments by Cleburne and Maney, retreating toward higher ground at Bald Hill. In some instances, the Federals protected themselves by fighting from first one side of their entrenchments and than the other, depending on the direction of the attack. First Lieutenant Edmund Nutt of the 20th Ohio Volunteer Infantry described the hand-to-hand melee that he experienced that day:

> The tree protection gave the Johnnies the advantage of the trench side of our works, and we have to take the other side. Over we went, jumping down on them and mingling with slash and clash. With yells we rushed along the line, taking them in and ordering them over on our side and to pass down the line; recapturing our own boys whom they

were holding as prisoners, and thus passing through and among them, neither daring to fire as we were all mixed together. Several of these raids were made during the afternoon, and the intermediate time was occupied in crouching to load and reaching over to fire.[153]

Toward dark, the 20th Ohio retired a few hundred yards to Leggett's Hill (Bald Hill), to a fort of earth and logs that faced east and south. Here they held on until the firing stopped at midnight.

Brigadier General Mortimer Leggett, commanding the 3rd Division, XVII Corps that day, was a Quaker with strict moral convictions, never drinking, smoking, or using profane language. Drinking liquor and playing cards at his headquarters was strictly forbidden. His troops named Bald Hill, "Leggett's Hill" in his honor after the fighting on 22 July. A photograph taken in 1893, twenty-nine years after the battle, shows mounds of earth—all that remains of the works of Leggett's trenches on Bald Hill. Most of this hill has disappeared to the construction of an access ramp to I-20 forty years ago. Today, a few blocks away on McPherson Avenue, is the "inverted-gun" monument marking the site of the death of Major General James B. McPherson, the only army commander killed in the war.[154]

The Battle of Atlanta on 22 July, ended with the Confederates abandoning their gains and on the next day, returning to the Atlanta fortifications. Hardee and Cheatham claimed the capture of thirteen artillery guns and nineteen battle flags. Their casualties that day exceeded 7,000, with the Federals listing theirs as about 5,000. General Bragg telegraphed President Davis that a great victory had been won. In a few days, with the Confederates having abandoned the trenches won, and back in the fortifications of Atlanta where they had started, no one was calling 22 July a victory. Whatever the fruits of victory Hood may have claimed, all knew the Confederacy was 7,000 casualties poorer for its efforts at Bald Hill that day.

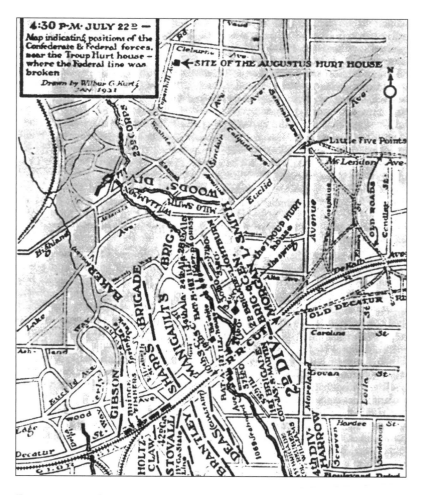

This Kurtz battle map shows troop positions and actions at the Confederate breakthrough at the railroad cut late in the afternoon of 22 July 1864. This action is depicted well in the Cyclorama painting.

THE BATTLE
OF EZRA CHURCH

Continuing their engineering accomplishments, the Federals had the Western and Atlantic railroad running to the camps of Thomas's army south of Peachtree Creek by 25th of July. Colonel Wright had repaired the high bridge across the Chattahoochee in six days. Meanwhile, McPherson's army on the 21st had broken the Augusta railroad which enters Atlanta from the east, and the defeat on 22 July had erased all Confederate hopes of supplies and reinforcements from that direction. Sherman knew that by cutting the remaining two railroads entering Atlanta, the West [Point] RR from Montgomery, and the Macon & Western from Macon, Atlanta must capitulate.

So on 25 July Sherman ordered the Army of the Tennessee to move by successive corps from the left (from their position astride the Augusta RR) to the extreme right of the Federal army on the west side of town, in the direction of East Point. Here at East Point, the two remaining railroads shared a common route south for a few miles, the West Point RR then splitting away to the southwest toward Montgomery, while the Macon RR continued on to Macon. Meanwhile, the Federal cavalry under McCook and Stoneman, numbering about 6,000 troopers were to simultaneously destroy the Macon Railroad at Jonesboro (20 miles south of Atlanta). Stoneman, with 2,500 troopers, was given permission to go still further south to Andersonville in an effort to liberate the 30,000 Federal prisoners.

Dodge's XVI army corps on the 27th left its position on Leggett's Hill, marched near the Army of the Cumberland's trenches in front of the Atlanta fortifications, taking a new position to the west, facing east on the Elliott's Mill Road leading to Ezra Church. Blair's XVII army corps got into position on the right of Dodge early morning, extending the Federal line almost to Ezra Church on 28 July. Logan's XV army corps, fresh from the heavy battles on 22 July, took a position to the rear of Blair facing almost due south near the church, within sight of a well used road. This road, the Lickskillet, crossed Elliott's Mill Road here at right angles leading directly to the village on the river with that odd name, Lickskillet. Near this road-crossing was a strong salient of the city's Confederate fortifications protecting the railroads at East Point. On the 28th, Blair's right was within a mile of those railroads. The Confederates realized this threat to their lifeline, and were already constructing an extension from the salient:

> Running southwest some four miles, crossing the north fork of Utoy Creek, and resting on some very commanding hills with broken ground in front, near where runs the road from Atlanta to that same Sandtown on the Chattahoochee which gave the name to the off-mentioned road north of the river. The course of this line diverged somewhat from the railway, so that at the Sandtown road it was nearly two miles away. Johnston's plans at Marietta were to be substantially repeated, and the warfare of flanking lines was to be prolonged to East Point.[155]

Here at Ezra Church, the third battle for Atlanta would take place. The Confederates under Major General S. D. Lee, supported by two divisions of Stewart's, deployed along Lickskillet Road and advanced to the attack. The attack struck Logan's XV army corps at the point it bent back at right angles from Blair's corps near Ezra Church. The Confederate attack was flawed from the start. With divisions attacking by brigades in a series of uncoordinated efforts, it was a failing effort. Although caught before they could entrench, the Federals had no problem repulsing these attacks, and became better fortified during the day as they continued entrenching between attacks. Many of the Confederate general officers, finding the willingness of the soldiers to continue attacking lessening as the day wore on sought unsuccessfully to encourage their men. Federal skirmishers could clearly see: "In the last attacks portions of the command refus[ing] to advance, and line officers with their drawn swords were seen from our works to march to the front of troops that would not follow them."[156]

The battle of Ezra Church was Hood's third major defeat in eight days. At this point the commander who had so criticized his predecessor for not being aggressive, now returned his battered army to the safety of the city fortifications. The siege of Atlanta was underway—the Confederate army weaker by nearly 20,000 casualties.

ATLANTA UNDER SIEGE:
SHELL AND SHOT

The first three weeks in August brought the full fury of the siege to Atlanta. On 19 July, Sherman had ordered his army commanders to halt "once they reached cannon and musket range of the city." Should they be fired upon by either cannon or rifles from the forts or buildings of Atlanta, "no consideration must be paid to the fact that they are occupied by families, but the place must be cannonaded without the formality of a demand [for surrender]."[157]

Virtually every house along Marietta Street was soon leveled by the bombardment. The railroad depot and the business center of town were selected as special Federal targets. To add to the havoc, Sherman brought a number of large siege guns from Chattanooga that were capable of lobbing 4 1/2-inch diameter shells weighing over 80 pounds into the heart of the city.[158] The Confederates had eight siege guns of their own. These guns had been brought from the coast, and fired shells weighing nearly 100 pounds, measuring 6.4 inches in diameter. Because of the rush of air when these shells came nearby, they called them "camp kettles." In his journal, Private Benjamin Smith of the 51st Illinois Infantry Regiment told of seeing one of these Confederate guns fire a shell directly at his nearby division headquarters. Private Smith described his experience:

Over in Atlanta they have planted one of their heaviest guns. It being on a slight elevation we can see it without the aid of a glass; with outlooks stationed on the top of a high building they signal to their gunner, how to point the gun so as to do the most damage.... While one of the boys and myself stood talking together...a big camp kettle from this gun came along and passed a few feet above our heads, making the most infernal noise as it cut through the air. We felt the wind from its swift rush as it passed; turning our eyes we saw it strike the side of a tree just below us, taking out a chunk half its size; exploding, it smashed the rear in of one of our wagons and killed a mule that was tied to it.[159]

Long after the war, Mollie Smith, a young lady in her mid-twenties during that hot summer of siege in Atlanta, remembered the terror of seeing the nightly flashes of the big guns, hearing their loud reports, and observing the paths of fiery shells, hissing and shrieking across the sky as they arched over the roof tops of the darkened town to land with a sickening crash among the houses. To Mollie, writing in the 1920s, the memory of the terrifying screams that followed the explosion of many of these shells would never be forgotten. It was indeed miraculous that only

(left) The shell fragments contained in these two bins are but a small sample that could be gathered from Atlanta streets after the six-week siege of the city in 1864. (right) Most of these 10,000 minie balls were discovered by the author in campsites and battlefields of the Atlanta Campaign. Sherman's official ammunition report lists more than 22 million rounds of small-arm ammo expended during the campaign. With the smaller Confederate army surely expending two-thirds of that amount during the same period, a great deal of lead was left on the ground. Much of it is now in private collections.

This sketch (probably by Theodore Davis) shows one of many "bomb proofs" in which Atlanta citizens sought shelter during Sherman's artillery blitz during July and August 1864.

twenty civilian deaths were estimated to have resulted from the thousands of such missiles hurled into the city. Atlantans learned to live with these dangers during that summer. There was remarkably little panic after the first few days of shelling.[160] Families subsisted on the products from their gardens prudently planted in the spring. While they gathered food from one corner of their backyards, they constructed bomb shelters (See above sketch.) in another corner of the same lot. By "bombs" they meant of course artillery shells. The bomb proofs were usually single-room dugouts in the ground with a ceiling of logs or heavy planking covered with two or three feet of packed earth and usually entered by a single door. The shelters were often shared by two or more families for hours at a time. The occupants of these bomb proofs came to expect sudden visits from passersby, often total strangers, who descended into their midst and remained until a lull in the bombardment. After this brief interlude in which all shared the common danger, these strangers departed, often never to be seen again by the family.[161]

Meanwhile, the entrenchment race for the railroads at East Point continued. The troop morale of the Confederates had been badly damaged by the defeats of the 20, 22, and 28 July. In a classic exchange between rival pickets shortly thereafter, the Yank asked the Reb, "Well Johnny, how many more of you are left?" The reply came, "Oh about

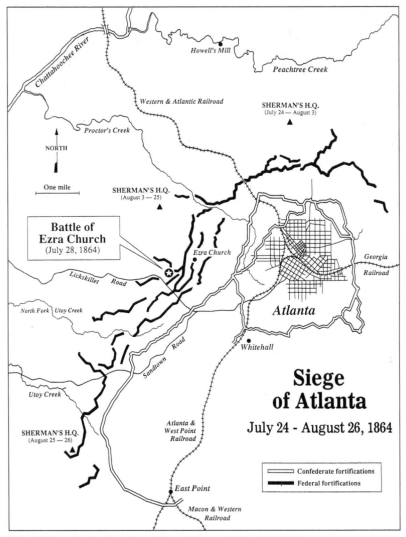

Map of Sherman's siege lines about Atlanta (Courtesy William R. Scaife.)

enough for another killing," characterizing the depth of this frustration. Between 6 and 8 August, several battles along the branches of Utoy Creek were fought, generally favorable to the Confederates, but causing them eventually to bend their entrenchments along a line of hills near the "north fork of Utoy Creek, southward across the Sandtown road about a mile and a half, thence bending a little toward the east follow[ing] the hilly ridges behind the southernmost branches of Utoy Creek till it reached the railway a mile beyond East Point."[162]

The West Point Railroad was now cut, leaving only the line to Macon unobstructed. Here, since the Confederates could entrench as fast as the Federals could, always leaving the lifeline to Macon protected, Sherman decided that a more daring strategy must be employed, but first he would try a cavalry raid on the railroad near Jonesboro. McCook and Stoneman would lead.

THE FAILURES
OF SHERMAN'S CAVALRY

Throughout the Atlanta Campaign, the Southern cavalry had been more than a match for their Federal counterparts. Wheeler had led his rebel troopers brilliantly at Pickett's Mill, at Cass Station, and at the McAfee Crossroads, near the Canton Road in Cobb County. On one occasion, exasperated by the timidity of his cavalry, Sherman had preemptory ordered Garrard to cross Noonday Creek on the Canton road and tangle seriously with Wheeler, chiding Garrard that since his opponent could regularly cross big rivers like the Etowah, surely his Federal cavalry could cross the little creek at Noonday. Garrard did as ordered, and preceded then to get a thorough spanking from his more aggressive, though less well-armed and "fewer in number" opponent. The railroad raid to destroy the tracks near Jonesboro would be an opportunity for the Federal cavalry to prove itself to its commander. Instead, the raid was a total fiasco. For the Federals, everything that could go wrong went wrong. Stoneman's portion of the cavalry force failed to rendezvous on the appointed day with McCook's troopers at Jonesboro. McCook was where he was supposed to be, wrecking the Macon railroad near Jonesboro. Stoneman was near Macon where he was not supposed to be, off on a personal glory junket to free the prisoners at Andersonville. Upon failing to get across the river at Macon, Stoneman found himself fighting the battle of his life to save himself and his reputation at nearby

Sunshine Church. Believing, incorrectly, that he was vastly outnumbered, Stoneman surrendered to a smaller Confederate force, becoming himself a prisoner of war. He would learn later that only a few scattered remnants of his command using various routes, would return safely to Atlanta to tell the story of his incompetence and poor leadership. Meanwhile at Jonesboro, after waiting several days for Stoneman to rendezvous, and learning of the approach of Wheeler with an unknown number of hard-riding Confederates, McCook headed west for the Chattahoochee River and safety via Newnan. Near Newnan, at the battle of Brown's Mill, Wheeler overtook his opponent, completely routing him with the aid of a small contingent of Southern infantry that had just pulled into Newnan by rail the evening before from Alabama. McCook and some few of his command managed to cross the Chattahoochee, and in a round-about ramble returned to Atlanta a week later. The McCook/Stoneman raid had cost more than 5,000 Federal casualties of all types, and the railroad was back in business forty-eight hours later. Sherman tried a final cavalry raid

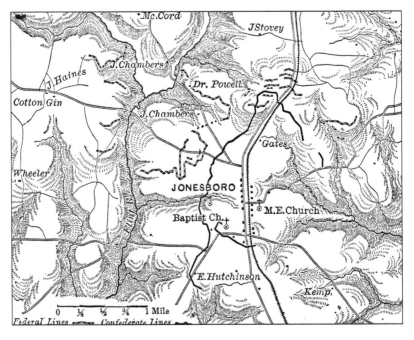

The Jonesboro battlefield with entrenched lines (Cox, *Atlanta*).

with hard-drinking and hard-cussing Major General Judson ("killcavalry") Kilpatrick leading, with no better success than previous efforts although Kilpatrick did return intact. The railroad to Macon, supposedly damaged severely was repaired again within two days.

Sherman became convinced that cavalry either would not or could not do severe damage to a railroad. He would use his infantry next time.

FLANKING TO JONESBORO:
ATLANTA IS LOST

On Thursday, 25 August 1864, dawn broke on a strangely quiet Atlanta. Since an evening late in May when S. P. Richards and neighbors heard the far away rumble of artillery echoing from the rocky, pine-covered hills of a place called New Hope Church, the sound of battle had been a constant companion. Now the silence seemed strange. Within a few hours word was received that the Union trenches were deserted. Many said that Sherman, frustrated by the carefully constructed defenses so expertly designed by Colonel L. P. Grant of the Confederate engineers, had given up his efforts to capture Atlanta. Richards was not so sure. On the following Monday, Richards and his wife Sallie strolled out of cannon-wrecked Marietta Street to the abandoned Union lines and marveled at the strength of these fortifications. Richard's fears concerning Sherman's plans soon proved well-founded, for the wily Union commander had marched his infantry in a wide flanking sweep south to the little railroad hamlet of Jonesboro which was located astride the Macon railroad some 20 miles south of Atlanta.[163] The last battles in the Atlanta Campaign were fought at Jonesboro on 31 August and 1 September. Hood, completely fooled by this audacious maneuver, entirely lost the 80,000–man Federal army for four days. Hearing that "some enemy infantry may be near Jonesboro on the railroad," Hood sent Hardee to Jonesboro to "drive them away." Hardee's efforts failed to dislodge the

Federals west of the tracks, and then, making matters worse, Hood, now thoroughly confused, recalled one third of Hardee's force to Atlanta on the evening of the 31st. Now Hardee must fight the next day's battle against a veteran army outnumbering him 5 to 1.

The 1 September battle for Jonesboro was fought on the north and west side of town along the railroad. Hardee's line stretched some distance across the railroad to the east, then to the west side of the tracks, the line looping around the Warren House, then running some distance in a southerly direction sufficient to cover the depot. Impossibly outnumbered, Hardee lost nearly 3,000 prisoners. Had it not been for Sherman's own ineptness in attacking in a timely fashion, Hardee's escape with a majority of his army under cover of the night would not have been possible. A new Confederate line a few miles south of Jonesboro at Lovejoy was established during the night. With the last railroad to Atlanta destroyed, Hood must now abandon the city.

On the evening of 1 September, as the last columns of the Army of Tennessee left Atlanta, disappearing in the dust and darkness of McDonough Street, citizens nearby heard the soldiers signing a song called "Lorena." The haunting lyrics told of happier moments of springtime and love in a faraway home before the coming of war's destruction. Romantic and sentimental, the song described a world that had never really existed and the promise of a future that now could never be. The darkness that concealed the last of the Confederate soldiers that hot September evening on McDonough Street was in effect a curtain closing on a way of life.[164]

Portions of Sherman's army entered Atlanta on 2 September. The news of Atlanta's surrender electrified the North into an orgy of week-long celebrations, and assured the reelection of Abraham Lincoln that fall. The next few weeks brought the hardships of Federal occupation to the people of Atlanta. Determined to make Atlanta a garrison town, Sherman ordered all civilians from the city; they must either go through the lines to waiting Confederate wagons south of the city at the village of Rough and Ready, or go north by rail (compliments of Sherman) to Yankee friends. Thus many like the Northern-born Richard's family found shelter and comfort above the Mason-Dixon line.

This sketch depicts Federal troops tearing down war-damaged Atlanta homes. The final destruction of Atlanta came the night of 16 November 1864, when fires and explosives destroyed about 80 percent of Atlanta before Sherman began his march to the sea *(Courtesy of Echoes of Battle)*.

Lizzie Perkerson, a young Atlantan writing a letter in September to a brother in Virginia, told of the difficulty of obtaining food and medicine in a country occupied by Federal soldiers. The Perkersons' home just 3 miles outside Atlanta, was the frequent victim of Union foraging parties. Since the Perkersons chose to remain in their home rather than take flight, sympathetic Federal officers spared their house from the torch that destroyed two thirds of Atlanta in November.[165] Just as time and effort removed the scars of war from the city, so the passing years healed the deep wounds of hate and bitterness in those who had experienced the ordeal of battle that summer in 1864. After the war Lizzie Perkerson married one of her "despised" Yankees and lived for many years in New York. She returned to Atlanta following the death of her husband and died at the age of ninety-seven in the house in which she had written the letter to her brother more than seventy years before.[166]

And so the people of Atlanta experienced war. Most had fled the city before the enemy arrived, but those who remained usually bore the dangers of war with fortitude. The quality that most characterized the conduct of Atlanta's civilians from January to September 1864 was their insistence upon going about customary activities despite the pressures of the military emergency. Patriotism was not the primary reason for this resoluteness. Most of those remaining in town did so because they really had no place to go. For these, staying was better than certain homelessness. At the moment the choice to stay seemed the best in a world of bad alternatives.

SHERMAN'S TRAIL
OF BATTLE IN RETROSPECT

A nd so ends our journey along the 1864 trail of battle to Atlanta. Today residential and commercial developments are rapidly changing the visual experience of this once-wild and rural route. The battlefield of New Hope Church is a case on point. Photographs taken four years ago in preparation for this book show road patterns and rural life near the church crossroads much the same as in 1864. Today (2006) the road intersection has been shifted a hundred yards eastward, and new residential subdivisions intrude on the Hell Hole ravine as well as the gun fort of the Cherokee Battery south of the crossroads. A major shopping mall, sporting a large Publix grocery store, now occupies much of the battlefield near General Polk's headquarters at the New Hope Church crossroads. The historic cemetery and the WPA pocket park are all that remain to remind us of the history at this spot. Southeast of New Hope Church is the 100-acre Pickett's Mill Battlefield state reservation.

In Cobb County, a few miles distance from Pickett's mill, is the Kennesaw National Battlefield 3000-acre reservation, now engulfed in a sea of Atlanta sprawl. Beyond Kennesaw Mountain there is little left of the 1864 scene. The pace of residential and commercial development is relentless and so intense that in the two years it has taken to write this book miles of military entrenchments and cannon forts have been swept away to make room for the flood of newcomers engulfing the county.

Recently the Dixon House, a rare survivor among the many war-scarred houses that once marked Sherman's battle route to Atlanta, was scheduled for immediate demolition to make room for yet another residential subdivision. At the last possible hour, Cobb County officials became convinced through the efforts of a few heritage-minded citizens that a public landmark was about to be destroyed (due partially to a county planning oversight) and ordered the Dixon House moved to nearby county property at public expense on 22 December 2005. At best a partial victory for historic heritage—the 200-year-old oak tree nearby could not be moved.

Around Atlanta, historical markers and the remarkable Cyclorama painting depicting the 1864 Battle of Atlanta are all that remain. Away from Atlanta, there is still much to see of the historic environment along the battle trail north of New Hope Church. Frequently, forested mountain ridges and many jungle ravines remain much as they appeared in 1864. Today, back roads take you to the more remote battle and camp sites described in this narrative. So, for the adventurous spirit there is certain satisfaction to be gained in this fascinating journey along the 1864 path of the battle to Atlanta.

So, in our journey down the battle path, we should honor the emotional cost to that wartime generation. In the closing scenes of late summer 1864, the 63rd Georgia was disbanded, decimated by the hardships of battle in the campaign. Mercer's entire brigade no longer existed, virtually wiped out in the 22 July Battle of Atlanta. General Mercer returned to Savannah having been retired to inactive service because of infirmities of "old age." And the "Old Captain," Charles Wallace Howard, was admitted to the military hospital in Macon in November 1864. Wounded twice during the course of the campaign, and in failing health, Howard took the required pledge of loyalty to the United States in May 1865. Returning home the same summer, he turned over the operation of the private school at Spring Bank to his daughters and devoted his last years to scientific research and writing. He traveled widely on horseback, and in 1867 he published a series of articles in a Bartow County newspaper concerning the "Condition and the Resources of Georgia." Reverend Howard died on Christmas day 1876. He is buried in the family cemetery at Spring Bank. Confederate General Johnston commenting on the death of his friend Charles Wallace Howard: "His loss is a great one to Georgia. For his capacity, patriotism and virtue [were] made more truly useful, since the war, than any other Georgian. I valued his friendship as highly as any that I could claim, and I shall regret his death and cherish his memory during the remainder of my life.[167]

And so in Reverend Charles Wallace Howard, the "Old Captain," we find the example of a gentleman whose inclination and education was religion, his personal interest, academics. Yet he chose instead, despite advanced age and absence of formal military training, to set aside all this and become a soldier in an arduous and dangerous history-making war experience. Duty called and he felt compelled to respond. It can be said that he lived his life as a statement of personal character. In another sense, his life may be seen as a microcosm of the larger Southern experience in the American Civil War.

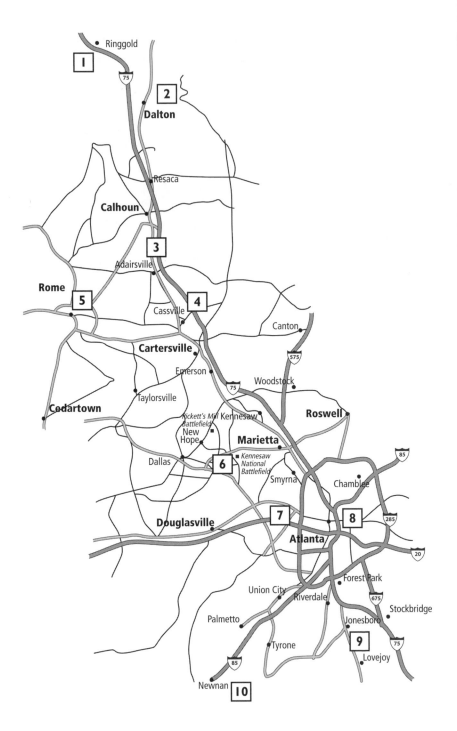

Appendix I

Sherman March Tour 1

1. Ringgold
Andrews Raid Marker • W&A Depot • Stone Church • Atlanta Campaign WPA Pocket Park

2. Dalton
Tunnel Hill • Clisby Austin House (Sherman's Headquarters) • Mill Creek Gap WPA Atlanta Campaign Marker—Ga. Highway Patrol Headquarters • Dalton RR Depot • Dug Gap Battlefield • Resaca Battlefield (Camp Creek state battle site) • Resaca Cemetery • W&A Railroad Bridge

Sherman March Tour 2

3. Adairsville
Site of "Octagon House" (Historical Marker) • W&A Depot in Adairsville • Site of "Spring Bank (Historical Marker & Cemetery)

4. Town of Cassville
Site of court house (WPA stone marker) • Cassville Cemetery • Dr. Hardy House

5. Rome
Noble Foundry Park

Sherman March Tour 3

6. Lost Mountain
Kennesaw Hill battlefield on Burnt Hickory Road

7. Johnston River Line

Sherman March Tour 4

8. Battles for Atlanta

Sherman March Tour 5

9. Jonesboro

Sherman March Tour 6

10. Battles of Browns Mill at Newnan (Historical Marker)

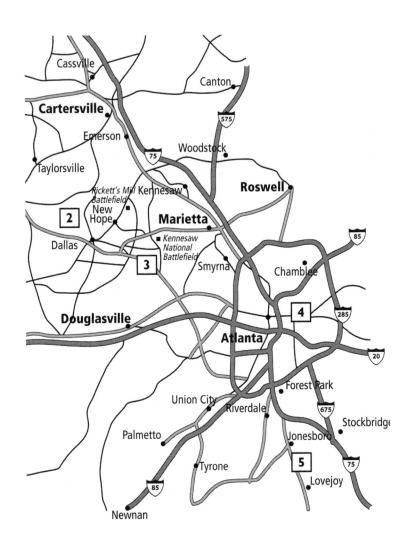

APPENDIX II

SHERMAN MARCH TOUR 2

New Hope Church Battlefield (WPA monument and tablet) • The "ravine" battle site (Sgt. Collin's death) • Confederate Cemetery at New Hope • Butterfield's entrenchments Pickett's Mill State Historic Site • Dallas Battlefield on the Villa Rica Road

SHERMAN MARCH TOUR 3

Site of Battle of Foster's Farm (Historical Marker) • Lost Mountain • Battle of Pine Knob Site of Death of Capt. Peter Simonson • Battlefield of Latimer's Farm (Latimer House & French's Hill) • Mud Creek battle lines on McDaniel Road and Dallas highway • Bald Hill battle ground (a.k.a. Artillery or Nodine's Hill) • Wallis House (on Burnt Hickory Road) • Battle of Kennesaw Mountain at Cheatham Hill • Battle of Ruff's Mill • Johnston River Line

SHERMAN MARCH TOUR 4

Battle of Peachtree Creek (Collier Road) • Battle Atlanta: Walker Monument (Glenwood Ave.) & McPherson Monument (McPherson Ave.) • Battle of Ezra Church (Historical Markers) Utoy Creek Siege Lines Park (Entrenchments & Historical Markers) • Cyclorama Painting (Grant Park)

SHERMAN MARCH TOUR 5

Battle of Jonesboro at Warren House (House & Historical Markers) • Battle of Jonesboro at Confederate Cemetery • Post-war Jonesboro Depot • Confederate Entrenchments (Lovejoy)

FOOTNOTES

1 US War Department, *The War of the Rebellion: A Compilation of the Official Records of the Union and Confederate Armies*, 128 vols. (Washington, DC: Government Printing Office, 1880–1901) ser. 1, vol. 38, pt. 3, p. 713 (hereinafter *Official Record*).

2 Jacob Dolson Cox, *Civil War Campaigns: Atlanta* (New York: Charles Scribner's Sons, 1882) 31.

3 *Official Records*, ser. 1, vol. 38, pt. 4, pp. 39–40.

4 *Official Records*, ser. 1, vol. 38, pt. 4, p. 25.

5 *Official Records*, ser. 1, vol. 38, pt. 4, p. 40.

6 The Henry rifle's under-barrel magazine can hold fifteen [text says 16] rim fire, .44 caliber cartridges, which could be fired in less than twelve seconds. The Henry was the most advanced repeating weapon in the war, but each rifle cost $35.00. Though far too expensive to be issued generally to the troops, the Henry was purchased privately by commanders for limited distribution in several Midwestern units such the 66th and 86th Illinois regiments. The Henry repeater evolved into the famed Winchester after the Civil War.

7 US War Department, *The War of the Rebellion: A Compilation of the Official Records of the Union and Confederate Armies*, 128 vols. (Washington, DC: Government Printing Office, 1880–1901) ser. 1, vol. 38, pt. 3, p. 378.

8 Clement Evans, *Confederate Military History*, 2 vols. (New York: Thomas Yoseloff Publishing, 1962) 6:100.

9 US War Department, *The War of the Rebellion: A Compilation of the Official Records of the Union and Confederate Armies*, 128 vols. (Washington, DC: Government Printing Office, 1880–1901) ser. 1, vol. 38, pt. 4, p. 715.

10 *Official Records*, ser. 1, vol. 38, pt. 4, p. 716.

11 *Official Records*, ser. 1, vol. 38, pt. 3, p. 420. Private Asabel M. Pyburn of Rice's brigade is credited with this accomplishment.

12 Henry Stone, "Opening the Campaign," in *The Atlanta Papers*, ed. Sidney C. Kerksis (Dayton OH: Morningside Press, 1980) 68.

13 Ibid.

14 James Barnes, et.al., *The 86th Regiment Indiana Volunteer Infantry* (Crawfordville IN: Journal Company Printers, 1895) 347.

15 Stephen Pierson, "From Chattanooga to Atlanta in 1864——A Personal Reminiscence," *Proceedings of the New Jersey Historical Society, A Quarterly Magazine* (July 1931): 13.

16 For instance, during the construction of I-75 near Calhoun GA, Ernest Rutledge of Resaca discovered a Civil War burial site in 1960 .

17 Ms. Mary J. Green, whose house was a battlefield landmark and a military hospital during the battle, was a tireless worker after the war in the search for Confederate graves. The Confederate Cemetery at Resaca is a monument to her leadership and energy.

18 Ernest Rutledge interview by Philip Secrist, 16 July 1997, typescript, Philip Secrist personal papers, Kennesaw GA. Friends of Resaca Battlefield added 65 additional acres in 2003 including the hilltop fort constructed by Georgia militia in 1862 to guard the railroad river crossing.

19 The Georgia legislature established the commission in 1993 at the request of Governor Zell Miller who was encouraged to do so by State Legislator John Carlisle and several other soon-to-be members of the GA Civil War Commission.

20 Jacob Dolson Cox, *Civil War Campaigns: Atlanta* (New York: Charles Scribner's Sons, 1882) 51.

21 Henry Stone, "Opening the Campaign," in *The Atlanta Papers*, ed. Sidney C. Kerksis (Dayton OH: Morningside Press, 1980) 70.

22 Ibid.

23 Cox, *Atlanta*, 60–61.

24 Ibid. See examples of Sherman's mapping product on page 24, as seen in the *Official Atlas of the American Civil War*.

25 Sam Watkins, *Co Aytch; A Side Show of the Big Show* (New York: Collier Books Pub., 1962) 149–51.

26 Ibid. The Octagon House was destroyed the next day. Today there is an historical marker across the road. Bricks from the house may still be found at the site.

27 Frances Howard, *In and Out of the Lines* (Cartersville GA: Etowah Valley Historical Society, 1997) 12, 13, 15–17.

28 Ibid.

29 Ibid. Col. R. G. Earle commanded this Alabama cavalry unit. His remains are buried in this courtyard.

30 Howard, *In and Out of the Lines*, 27. Wilbur Kurtz provided the research for tracing the march route to Barnsley's of the XIII and XVI corps. Kurtz, a native of Illinois and a well-known author, artist, and historian, was a long-time resident of Atlanta. He served as technical advisor for the movie *Gone With the Wind* at the request of Margaret Mitchell. His maps of the Atlanta Campaign are well researched and beautifully drawn. The Wilbur Kurtz Papers are in the Atlanta History Center collection.

31 Howard, *In and Out of the Lines*, pp.28-30. There is an excellent chapter about the history of Godfrey Barnsley's Woodlands in Medora Perkerson's *White Columns in Georgia*. The Barnsley house furnishings were auctioned in 1941 and remain scattered throughout Georgia and beyond. Two sets of magnificent bedroom furnishings—two beds, two mirrored vanities, and an armoire—are in the possession of the author. The top of one vanity contains a bullet scar from the murder of a Barnsley descendent in the 1930s.

32 Frances Howard, *In and Out of the Lines* (Cartersville GA: Etowah Valley Historical Society, 1997) 1.

33 Lucy Cunyas, *History of Bartow County, Georgia* (Easley, SC, Tribune Publishing Company, 1933]) 290. The public is indebted to Professor J. B. Tate, Kennesaw State University, for his preservation activities at Spring Bank.

34 See the Kurtz troop march and location route map of Cassville area. Hooker's XX army corps was to strike the railroad near Cass Station, cutting off retreat to the Etowah River, effectively trapping the Confederate army.

35 US War Department, *The War of the Rebellion: A Compilation of the Official Records of the Union and Confederate Armies*, 128 vols. (Washington, DC: Government Printing Office, 1880–1901) ser. 1, vol. 38, pt. 3, p. 953.

36 Research through the years indicate that the troops who spooked Hood that day at Cassville was a division of Federal cavalry that happened to be east of town. It should have posed no real threat to the Confederate infantry attack plan.

37 *Official Records*, ser. 1, vol. 38, pt. 3, p. 984.

38 See accompanying Kurtz map of the Cassville battlefield.

39 William T. Sherman, *Memoirs of W. T. Sherman*, 2 vols. (Charles L. Webster, 1875). Also, Clement Evans, *Confederate Military History*, 2 vols. (New York: Thomas Yoseloff Publishing, 1962) 6:308.

40 Sherman, *Memoirs of W. T. Sherman*, 2:127. It was on this occasion that Sherman suggested Hill carry a message to Georgia governor Brown proposing that the state of Georgia secede from the Confederacy by withdrawing its troops from action. While the governor did disband the state militia on his own initiative, Sherman's proposal of "secession" from the Confederacy was never seriously considered. Also, Evans, *Confederate Military History*, 6:308.

41 Jenkins Lloyd Jones, *An Artilleryman's Diary* (Madison WI: Wisconsin State Historical Society, 1914). Jones was probably on the campus of the Baptist Male College since there was no observatory at the Cassville Female College.

42 Lucy Cunyas, *History of Bartow County, Georgia* (Easley SC: Tribune Publishing Company, 1933) 234.

43 Information obtained at the town site by Joseph B. Mahan, Jr., in 1950 as a partial requirement for MA degree at University of Georgia. From these measurements, Mahan created the street and block map of Cassville (Joseph B. Mahan, Jr., *A History of Old Cassville, 1833–1864* [Cartersville GA: Etowah Valley Historical Society, 1998] 28).

44 Mahan, *A History of Old Cassville*, 44.

45 Ibid., 47.

46 Ibid., 34. Several undocumented reasons have been given for the railroad construction bypassing Cassville. One such explanation contends that leaders in town did not want the noise and "baggage" associated with a railroad to disturb the cultural atmosphere of their village. The explanation concerning topography and cost of construction given in John H. Johnston's *History of the Western and Atlantic Railroad* (44–45) seems more plausible.

47 J. L. Milholllin, interview by Joseph B. Mahan, Jr., quoted in Mahan, *A History of Old Cassville*, 31.

48 "Lizzie Gaines' Journal," *Northwest Georgia Historical & Genealogical Quarterly*: 1. Frances Elizabeth Gaines was a resident of Cassville and an eyewitness on the day it was burned. Gaines kept a journal during the war. She was thirty-four years of age when the town was burned. After the war, she married Rev. Bethel Bryant Quillian. She died in 1900.

49 "Gaines' Journal," 6.

50 Reinforcements did arrive in June. Two divisions of Frank Blair's XVII army corps (Army of the Tennessee) arrived on 8 June from Huntsville AL—about 10,000 men.

51 *Official Records*, series 1, vol. 38, pt. 4, p. 507.

52 Henry Stone, "Opening the Campaign," in *The Atlanta Papers*, ed. Sidney C. Kerksis (Dayton OH: Morningside Press, 1980) 60–61.

53 The railroad towns and villages destroyed in November included Atlanta, Marietta, Acworth, Cartersville, Kingston, Adairsville, and Calhoun. The destruction by fire or explosives of standing structures in these villages by Federal soldiers was typically 80–90 percent. (See letter from Confederate military official to Georgia governor Brown concerning conditions in Atlanta two weeks after Sherman's departure from Atlanta on the "March to the Sea").

54 *Official Records*, ser. 1, vol. 38, pt. 4, p. 579.

55 *Official Records*, ser. 1, vol. 38, pt. 4, p. 579.

56 *Official Records*, ser. 1, vol. 38, pt. 4, p. 579.

57 Ibid., pt. 4, p. 297–98.

58 Letter to Joseph E. Brown, 7 December 1864.

59 Connecting at Kingston with the mainline Western and Atlantic, the spur railroad to Rome GA was built in the 1850s. This railroad made possible the shipping of cotton and other goods by rail to Atlanta enhancing Rome's status as an inland river port. The tracks of the now-abandoned Rome line were in use until after World War II.

60 Medora Perkerson, *White Columns in Georgia* (New York: Bonanza Books, 1932) 204.

61 Perkerson, *White Columns in Georgia,* 199.

62 Perkerson, *White Columns in Georgia,* 204. This "cannonball story" is likely local fiction since the Federal army was amply supplied by rail with artillery ammunition throughout the Atlanta Campaign. Additionally, the Cooper Ironworks (where the cannonballs from the iron balustrade were said to have been made) located on the north bank of the Etowah River nearby had been destroyed completely the day after the Confederates retreated across the river.

63 Perkerson, *White Columns in Georgia,* 193.

64 Perkerson, *White Columns in Georgia,* 194.

65 Perkerson, *White Columns in Georgia,* 194.

66 Perkerson, *White Columns in Georgia,* 198.

67 Perkerson, *White Columns in Georgia,* 198.

68 Jacob Dolson Cox, *Civil War Campaigns: Atlanta* (New York: Charles Scribner's Sons, 1882) 61.

69 Ibid.

70 H. J. Lee, "The Battle of New Hope Church," *Confederate Veteran Magazine,* vol. 31 (February 1923): 61–62.

71 Curiously, and almost eerie in coincidence, a version of the 1864 horror in these woods and fields happened more than a century later with the fatal crash of a commercial airliner attempting an emergency landing on a nearby highway in a hailstorm in the very heart of this New Hope Civil War "field of battle."

72 Richard Baumgartner and Larry Strayer, eds., *Echoes of Battle: The Atlanta Campaign* (Huntington WV: Blue Acorn Press, 1991) 100.

73 Jacob Dolson Cox, *Civil War Campaigns: Atlanta* (New York: Charles Scribner's Sons, 1882) 68–69. Residential development near New Hope Church has significantly impacted this battle site since 2000. Most of the battlefield has been lost except 4 acres of ravines near the Cartersville Road saved through efforts of the Georgia Civil War Commission, 15 acres of battle trenches across the road owned by the Atlanta History Center, and the WPA memorial at the New Hope crossroads at the church.

74 US War Department, *The War of the Rebellion: A Compilation of the Official Records of the Union and Confederate Armies,* 128 vols. (Washington, DC: Government Printing Office, 1880–1901) ser. 1, vol. 38, pt. 3, p. 843.

75 *Official Records,* ser. 1, vol. 38, pt. 3, p. 843.

76 *Official Records,* ser. 1, vol. 38, pt. 3, p. 843.

77 The New Hope Church cemetery contains several Confederate graves from this battle. Gravesites are carefully marked, with the St. Andrews Cross battle flag flying overhead. Stoval's brigade of Stewart's division occupied the battle line in the cemetery.

78 *Official Records,* ser. 1, vol. 38, pt. 2, p. 123–24.

79 Alexander P. Stewart, "Stewarts' Division At New Hope Church," *Confederate Veteran Magazine,* vol. 5 (May 1897): 460. Also see in this same issue, a wartime poem about the Bridgen brothers (Fenner's Battery) heroic action here at New Hope Church.

80 Ibid.

81 H. J. Lee, "New Hope Church," *Confederate Veteran Magazine,* vol. 31 (February 1923): 62.

82 H. J. Lee, "General Stewart at New Hope Church," *Confederate Veteran Magazine,* vol. 38 (September 1930): 247.

83 Baumgartner and Strayer, eds., *Echoes of Battle,* 105.

84 Ibid., 104.

85 Ibid.

86 Stephen Pierson," From Chattanooga to Atlanta in 1864," in *The Atlanta Papers*, ed. Sidney C. Kerksis (Dayton OH: Morningside Press, 1980) 277.

87 *Official Records*, ser. 1, vol. 38, pt. 2, p. 124. Butterfield's division, though not connected with Geary's left at dawn on 26 May, was entrenched in the woods only a few hundred yards to the east. The two divisions linked their trenches later that morning. These Butterfield trenches are still visible today on a 15-acre wooded tract owned by the Atlanta Historical Society. In 2001, the Georgia Historical Commission acquired almost 5 acres of battlefield ravines near Geary's position during 25–26 May 1864.

88 R. M. Collins, *Chapters from the Unwritten History of the War Between the States* (St. Louis: Nixon-Jones Printing Company, 1893) quoted in Dennis McInvale, *The Battle of Pickett's Mill: Foredoomed to Oblivion* (Atlanta: Georgia Department of National Resources, 1971)

89 US War Department, *The War of the Rebellion: A Compilation of the Official Records of the Union and Confederate Armies*, 128 vols. (Washington, DC: Government Printing Office, 1880–1901) ser. 1, vol. 38, pt. 3, p. 750.

90 The battlefield at Pickett's Mill remains a valuable secluded outdoor classroom today. On one occasion nearly forty years ago, a high school group, seated quietly in the woods near the site of Grandbury's old battle line, found themselves the unexpected target of a bayonet charge by a concealed group of uniformed Civil War re-enactors. Those young people will forever remember the Battle of Pickett's Mill.

91 Tom Murphy to George Bagby, 11 August 1973, Georgia Department of Natural Resources files, Atlanta GA.

92 George Bagby memoes, Georgia Department of Natural Resources file, Atlanta GA. | Robin Jackson to George Bagby (memo) 15 August 1973, Georgia Department of Natural Resources file, Atlanta GA.

93 Much of the research and some of the writing in this chapter is credited to Jeff Frederick, a history major at Kennesaw State University in 2000. Frederick's work was done to meet the requirements of a senior thesis. This choice of topic was result of Frederick's interest in the Pickett's Mill battle site.

94 Richard Baumgartner and Larry Strayer, eds., *Echoes of Battle: The Atlanta Campaign* (Huntington WV: Blue Acorn Press, 1991) 126.

95 US War Department, *The War of the Rebellion: A Compilation of the Official Records of the Union and Confederate Armies*, 128 vols. (Washington, DC: Government Printing Office, 1880–1901) ser. 1, vol. 38, pt. 3, pp. 315–16.

96 *Official Records*, ser. 1, vol. 38, pt. 3, p. 163.

97 Account Pvt. John K. Duke, Co. F, 53rd Ohio, in Richard Baumgartner and Larry Strayer, eds., *Echoes of Battle: The Atlanta Campaign* (Huntington WV: Blue Acorn Press, 1991) 124–25.

98 Jacob Dolson Cox, *Civil War Campaigns: Atlanta* (New York: Charles Scribner's Sons, 1882) 86.

99 Editor's comments on Fulton County Superior Court meeting, *Atlanta Southern Confederacy*, 29 January 1864, Atlanta History Center Archives, Atlanta GA; Editor's comments on Atlanta City Council meeting, *Atlanta Southern Confederacy*, 2 February 1864, Atlanta History Center Archives, Atlanta GA.

100 Franklin M. Garrett, *Atlanta and Environs*, 2 vols. (Athens: University of Georgia Press, 1954) Vol. 1:569–70. Also, Atlanta article by Philip L. Secrist, "Life in Atlanta," *Civil War Times* July 7, 1970) pp. 9-12.

101 Editorial commenting on grand jury, *Atlanta Southern Confederacy*, 29 January 1864, n.p.

102 Minutes of the Fulton County Superior Court, 1864, book D, "Teenage Delinquincy."

103 Andrews was hanged near what is now Juniper Street, just behind the present day Georgian Terrace. The execution of the seven was on a common scaffold near Oakland Cemetery. The remains of all the raiders are now buried in a common plot in the Chattanooga National Military Cemetery.

104 Polk had maintained a personal correspondence with Jefferson Davis throughout the war and was often critical of other officers, and his failures at the battle of Chickamauga were well known. Today, an obelisk atop Pine Mountain marks the site of his death.

105 US War Department, *The War of the Rebellion: A Compilation of the Official Records of the Union and Confederate Armies*, 128 vols. (Washington, DC: Government Printing Office, 1880–1901) ser. 1, vol. 38, pt. 4, p. 776.

106 Hooker's XX army corps was the only corps in Sherman's army made up of Eastern regiments (i.e., New York, Connecticut, Pennsylvania, New Jersey, Maine, etc.). The majority of Sherman's army were mid-westerners. Hooker, commanding two depleted veteran corps, the XI and XII, had been sent from Virginia to Chattanooga in fall 1863 to help Grant drive the Confederates off Lookout Mountain and Missionary Ridge. The XI and XII corps remained in the Chattanooga area to participate later in the Atlanta Campaign. The two corps had been combined after Missionary Ridge into the new XX Army Corps, with Hooker continuing in command.

107 The Dixon House, Hooker's headquarters on 17 June, stands today on the Acworth-Due West Road. This bullet-riddled relic of the battle near Gilgal Church has been greatly remodeled over the years but remains as one of the few surviving Cobb County battle structures of the war. The Dixon House was moved in December 2005 to a new site to avoid demolition (See chap. 29.).

108 *Official Records*, ser. 1, vol. 38, pt. 2, p. 128.

109 In 2002, this area came under review for a proposed residential subdivision. Preservationists succeeded in persuading the developer to set aside almost 10 acres as a history preserve, including the 60th New York's entrenchments and the Confederate line of works.

110 *Official Records*, ser. 1, vol. 38, pt. 2, pp. 269–70.

111 *Official Records*, ser. 1, vol. 38, pt. 2, p. 270.

112 *Official Records*, ser. 1, vol. 38, pt. 2, p. 284.

113 *Official Records*, ser. 1, vol. 38, pt. 2, p. 150. Simonson's death-site is on the east side of Frank Kirk Road near the forks at the intersection with Kennesaw-Due West Road. The earthworks of the four-gun battery he was emplacing remain nearby.

114 This particular sniper was captured later that day and told the story of the two shots required to hit Simonson. The site of Simonson's death is known because of a four-gun battery fortification nearby, troop positions studies done by National Park Service historian Ed Bearss, and the recovery of an unfired (six-sided) Whitworth bullet at the spot occupied by the sniper (bullet recovered in 1995). Near the bullet recovery site were half a dozen impacted .58 caliber bullets indicating discovery of the sniper position too late to save Simonson. See photo of Whitworth bullet below.

115 *Official Records*, ser. 1, vol. 38, pt. 1, p. 223. Samuel French, *Two Wars: An Autobiography* (Confederate Veteran Press, Nashville, 1901) 203.

116 Since Polk's death on the 14th, Major General William Loring was in temporary command of that army.

117 US War Department, *The War of the Rebellion: A Compilation of the Official Records of the Union and Confederate Armies*, 128 vols. (Washington, DC: Government Printing Office, 1880–1901) ser. 1, vol. 38, pt. 1, p. 296. Also French's diary, Samuel French, *Two Wars: An Autobiography* (Confederate Veteran Press, Nashville, 1901) 203.

118 The firing position taken by the Spencer regiment was clearly marked in 1970 by the abundance of copper casings along that ridge. It was in this same location that three "short rounds" of artillery shells were also recovered.

119 Colonel Bartleson was killed by a sniper on 23 June near today's Dallas Highway western entrance to Kennesaw National Battlefield Park.

120 Cox, *Atlanta*, p. 101. This bluff at Mud Creek occupied by the Confederate fort was the recovery site of hundreds of Federal artillery shells and shell fragments in the 1960s and 1970s.

121 *Official Records*, ser. 1, vol. 38, pt. 1, p. 408.

122 *Official Records,* ser. I, vol. 4, pt. I, pp. 520-21. | Don Carnes (family historian and relative of the most recent owner) interview by author, 16 July 1994, typescript. The Wallis House survives today on its original site protected by preservation agreements with the nearby developer. Kennesaw National Battlefield Park superintendent John Cissell and Cobb County Commission Chairman Sam Olens took the lead in this action. The Wallis House itself has now been purchased through the joint efforts of the Georgia Civil War Commission and Cobb County government. The Wallis House is to be preserved and plans are that it will function eventually as a satellite site to the nearby Kennesaw National Battlefield Park. The crest of the historic signal hill behind the Wallis House is now owned by Cobb County.

123 A few years ago, a Confederate cannon barrel and carriage was recovered from this creek. Its whereabouts today remain a mystery. (Bill Kenney, editor for the *Marietta Daily Journal,* telephone converstation).

124 US War Department, *The War of the Rebellion: A Compilation of the Official Records of the Union and Confederate Armies,* 128 vols. (Washington, DC: Government Printing Office, 1880–1901) ser. I, vol. 38, pt. I, p. 243-45.

125 *Official Records,* ser. I, vol. 38, pt. I, pp. 243–44. The Confederate casualties are exaggerated.

126 The Bald Knob battlefield was rediscovered in the 1960s by the author. The hill is just west of the Kennesaw National Battlefield Park boundary. A mistake had been made by the National Park Service in the 1930s as to the location of "Nodine's Hill" (Bald Knob) listing it as *within* the park rather than just *outside* the park on private property owned by the Hayes family. Today, that record has been corrected and the NPS is actively trying to acquire the property. The knob came to be called "Artillery Hill" as a result of the trove of artillery artifacts recovered from that site over the years. See nearby photo of one such exhibit.

127 US War Department, *The War of the Rebellion: A Compilation of the Official Records of the Union and Confederate Armies,* 128 vols. (Washington, DC: Government Printing Office, 1880–1901) ser. I, vol. 38, pt. 2, pp. 548, 553.

128 US War Department, *The War of the Rebellion: A Compilation of the Official Records of the Union and Confederate Armies,* 128 vols. (Washington, DC: Government Printing Office, 1880–1901) ser. I, vol.38, pt. 3, p. 223.

129 Clement Evans, *Confederate Military History,* 2 vols. (New York: Thomas Yoseloff Publishing, 1962) 6:318–19.

130 *Official Records,* ser. I, vol. 38, pt. 4, pp. 799, 802.

131 After the battle, Zack Hoskins, a young rebel artilleryman standing nearby, witnessed the burial of a Federal lieutenant colonel behind the Confederate lines nearby. On 1 July, Sherman wrote a personal letter to Belle Barnhill, the widow, telling her of the bravery of her husband, that he had fallen too close to the enemy battle lines for his body to be recovered. Years later, Barnhill's only son read a newspaper story written by Hoskins describing the burial. The son, John Barnhill, contacted Hoskins, the two carrying on a written correspondence for many years relative to locating the site of his father's grave on Kennesaw Hill. Time passed, and for reasons unknown, the Confederate gunner and the son of a Yankee officer never met on the field to search for the lost grave on that hill in Cobb County.

132 Sam Watkins, *Co Aytch; A Side Show of the Big Show* (New York: Collier Books Pub., 1962) 158. The Lt. Col. Rigdon Barnhill story is the product of the good fortune of Civil War collector Newt Medford who discovered several of the Zach Hoskins letters recently. See nearby page for additional pictures and copies of items related to the story. Also see the reference to Barnhill's death in *Official Records,* ser. I, vol. 38, pt. 3, pp. 318, 323.

133 Sarah Temple, *First Hundred Years* (Atlanta: Walter Brown Press, 1938) 318. Col. William H. Martin, 1st Arkansas, is credited with this mid-battle truce.

134 Richard Baumgartner and Larry Strayer, eds., *Echoes of Battle: The Atlanta Campaign* (Huntington WV: Blue Acorn Press, 1991) 179. Sherman had been reluctant earlier to flank westward because of the danger of exposing his rail supply line to attack. By 1 July, he obviously had decided to risk this when he began his flanking movement west and south toward Smyrna in such a way as to force the Confederates to abandon their Kennesaw defenses to protect their rail connection to Atlanta.

135 Called the "Johnston River Line" and created by General Francis Shoupe (Johnston's chief of staff) with slave labor in early June 1864, this position was never attacked by Sherman's forces. Considered impregnable, the Federals simply bypassed these fortifications by river crossings eastward at Soap Creek and Roswell. Today, Cobb County owns a 100-acre remnant of this line. Planning will soon begin for trails and restoration of shoupades in this now-protected historic site.

136 Sarah Temple, *First Hundred Years* (Atlanta: Walter Brown Press, 1938) 325.

137 This Masonic building on the Marietta city square and the Manning mill on the Sandtown Road are two examples of the brotherhood of Masons in action during the war. Simpson Manning's Masonic literature found stored in his mill by the Federals, probably accounts for that structure's wartime survival.

138 The site of the Battle of Smyrna on 4 July became an issue in a public preservation controversy having to do with construction of a highway in the 1990s near the Ruff's Mill location. Some of the original mill buildings had survived the war, and an 1880-period covered bridge added further charm to the area. To strengthen their case concerning the opposition to the proximity of the proposed new highway at the mill, the preservationists mistakenly insisted that the Battle of Smyrna (sometimes called the Battle of Ruff's Mill) had been fought *at* the mill rather than the actual site 2 miles east at the Old Concord and Concord road intersections. Today there is a 100-acre history preserve protecting the mill and covered bridge environments. The actual site of the battle-field was lost long ago to a neighborhood of small homes and urban streets. Historical markers are in place.

139 US War Department, *The War of the Rebellion: A Compilation of the Official Records of the Union and Confederate Armies*, 128 vols. (Washington, DC: Government Printing Office, 1880–1901) vol. 38, pt. 3, 382. The Widow Mitchell house still stands near the Sandtown Road—built in 1836, it is Cobb County's oldest frame structure. In 2003, it has been offered by a developer-owner to any preservation group who will take possession and restore it.

140 *Official Records*, ser. 1, vol. 38, pt. 5, p. 76.

141 *Official Records*, ser. 1, vol. 38, pt. 5, p. 92. Thomas expressed concern for these Roswell women, telling Sherman that there was transportation for them only as far as Nashville, and adding that "it seems hard to turn them adrift." Sherman responded the same day to Thomas, telling him that General Webster in Nashville had been ordered to dispose of them by sending them to Indiana (*Official Records*, ser. 1, vol. 83, pt. 5, p. 104). Few of the "Roswell women" returned South after the war.

142 *Official Records*, ser. 1, vol. 38, pt..4, p. 108.

143 *Official Records*, ser. 1, vol. 38, pt. 4, p. 118.

144 Haywood J. Pearce, *Benjamin H. Hill* (Chicago: Charles Scribners Sons, 1928) 98.

145 L. P. Richard, "Richard's Diary," 24 May 1862. Atlanta History Center archives, Atlanta GA.

146 Editorial, *Atlanta Southern Confederacy*, 29 January 1864, n.p..

147 "Richard's Diary," 20 January 1864, n.p.

148 Ibid., 1 August 1864.

149 Wallace Reed, *Atlanta* (New York: Syracuse Press, 1889) 192.

150 Jacob Dolson Cox, *Civil War Campaigns: Atlanta* (New York: Charles Scribner's Sons, 1882) 156.

151 Clement Evans, *Confederate Military History*, 2 vols. (New York: Thomas Yoseloff Publishing, 1962) 6:329. An inverted-gun monument to Walker's death is in place near his death site on Glenwood Avenue.

152 Ibid. See picture of a portion of a Federal artillery shell found near the right of Walker's Confederate attackers.

153 Richard Baumgartner and Larry Strayer, eds., *Echoes of Battle: The Atlanta Campaign* (Huntington WV: Blue Acorn Press, 1991) 239.

154 This "inverted cannon" monument in this little park commemorating McPherson's death is surrounded by a small fence and well-tended flowers and shrubs, maintained by parties unknown. Walker's similar monument at nearby Glenwood Avenue has an appearance of neglect and disrepair.

155 Jacob Dolson Cox, *Civil War Campaigns: Atlanta* (New York: Charles Scribner's Sons, 1882) 183.

156 Cox, *Atlanta*, 185. Generals Stewart, Loring, Brown, and Johnson were wounded that day.

157 US War Department, *The War of the Rebellion: A Compilation of the Official Records of the Union and Confederate Armies*, 128 vols. (Washington, DC: Government Printing Office, 1880–1901) ser. 1, vol. 38, pt. 5, p. 193.

158 *Official Records*, ser. 1, vol. 38, pt. 5, pp. 448, 473.

159 Richard Baumgartner and Larry Strayer, eds., *Echoes of Battle: The Atlanta Campaign* (Huntington WV: Blue Acorn Press, 1991) 254. See nearby photograph of shells found near the Atlanta siege lines.

160 Wallace Reed, *Atlanta* (New York: Syracuse Press, 1889) 182.

161 Ibid., 183.

162 Cox, *Atlanta*, 193. In 2002, representatives of the Georgia Civil War Commission discovered and led the now-successful effort to preserve a section of the Federal siege line near Utoy Creek. The city of Atlanta, and a public-spirited philanthropist, joined with the commission to make this preservation triumph possible.

163 US War Department, *The War of the Rebellion: A Compilation of the Official Records of the Union and Confederate Armies*, 128 vols. (Washington, DC: Government Printing Office, 1880–1901) ser. 1, vol. 38, pt. 5, p. 482, 521.

164 A. A. Hoehling, *The Last Train From Atlanta* (New York: Charles Scribner's Sons, 1958) 406. Franklin M. Garrett, *Atlanta and Environs*, 2 vols. (Athens: University of Georgia Press, 1954) 1:633.

165 James R. Crew to his wife, 1 December 1864, James R. Crew Papers, Atlanta History Center. Also, see attached letter from Confederate General Howard to Governor Brown (1 December 1864) on Atlanta's destruction.

166 "Lizzie's Letter," *Atlanta Journal Magazine* (23 April 1944): 3, 10.

167 Anonymous, *Charles Wallace Howard* (pamphlet) (n.p., 1876). Pamphlet is in possession of Professor J. B. Tate, Etowah Valley Historical Society, Cartersville GA.

BIBLIOGRAPHY

Barnes, James, et.al. *The 86th Regiment Indiana Volunteer Infantry.* Crawfordville IN: Journal Company Printers, 1895.

Baumgartner, Richard and Larry Strayer, editors. *Echoes of Battle: The Atlanta Campaign.* Huntington WV: Blue Acorn Press, 1991.

Cox, Jacob Dolson. *Campaign of the Civil War: Atlanta.* Charles New York: Scribner's Sons, 1882.

Cunyas, Lucy J. *History of Bartow County, Ga.* Easley SC: Tribune Publishing Company, 1932.

Evans, Clement. *Confederate Military History.* 12 volumes. New York: Thomas Yoseloff Publishing Company, 1962.

French, Samuel. *Two Wars: An Autobiography.* Nashville: Confederate Veterans Press, 1904.

Garrett, Franklin M. *Atlanta and Environs.* 2 volumes. Athens: University of Georgia Press, 1954.

Hoehling, A. A. *The Last Train from Atlanta.* New York: Charles Scribner's Sons, 1985.

Howard, Frances. *In and Out of the Lines.* New York: Prentice Publishing Company, 1905.

Lloyd Jones, Jenkins. *An Artilleryman's Diary.* Madison WI: Wisconsin State Historical Society, 1914.

Kerksis, Sidney C., editor. *The Atlanta Papers.* Dayton OH: Morningside Press, 1980.

Lee, H. J. "The Battle of New Hope Church." *Confederate Veteran Magazine,* vol. 31 (February 1923): 61-62.

Lee, H. J. "General Stewart at New Hope Church," *Confederate Veteran Magazine,* vol. 31 (30 September 1930): 47.

McInvale, Morton R. *The Battle of Pickett's Mill—Foredoomed to Oblivion.* Atlanta: Georgia Department of National Resources, 1972.

Mahan, Jr., Joseph B. *A History of Old Cassville, 1833–1864.* Cartersville GA: Etowah Valley Historical Society, 1998.

Partridge, Charels A., editor. *History of the 96th Regiment Illinois Volunteer Infantry.* Chicago: (NFL), 1887.

Pearce, Haywood J. *Benjamin H. Hill.* Chicago: Charles Scribners Sons, 1928.

Pierson, Stephen. "From Chattanooga to Atlanta in 1864—A Personal Reminiscence," *Proceedings of the New Jersey Historical Society: A Quarterly Magazine* (July 1931): P. 27.

Perkerson, Medora. *White Columns in Georgia.* New York: Bonanza Books, 1932.

Reed, Wallace. *Atlanta.* New York: Syracuse Press, 1889.

Secrist, Phillip. "Life in Atlanta." *Civil War Times Illustrated* (July 1970):pp. 7-9.

Sherman, William T. *Memoirs of General William T. Sherman.* 2 volumes. New York: Charles L. Webster and Company, 1875.

Temple, Sarah G. *The First Hundred Years: A History of Cobb County, Georgia.* Atlanta: Walter W. Brown Press, 1938.

US War Department. *The War of the Rebellion: A Compilation of the Official Records of the Union and Confederate Armies.* 128 volumes. Washington, DC: Government Printing Office 1880–1901.

Watkins, Sam. *Co. Aytch: A Side Show of the Big Show.* New York: Collier Books Publishing, 1962.

INDEX